Contents

To my Dad, my mentor renegade.
I'm forever grateful that you took me straight to the top of
the double black diamond that day and made me skip
the bunny slope.

And to you, Mom, thank you for your constant
empowerment. You're the most positive person
I know. I love you both.

Foreword

Amy Jo Martin and I first "met" on Twitter when she was working with the Phoenix Suns. As luck would have it, I was scheduled to attend a conference in Phoenix a month or so later, so we ended up meeting at the conference, going on a hot air balloon ride (which the conference organizers had generously provided for all conference attendees), talked about the science of happiness over margaritas, and have remained friends ever since.

Soon after our first meeting in real life, Amy Jo let me know she was venturing out on her own. She decided to name her new company Digital Royalty, right around the time that my own book, *Delivering Happiness,* was about to come out. As we got to know each other better, we both realized that enlisting Digital Royalty's help for the book launch would be the perfect complement to our twenty-three-city nationwide book bus tour around the country in 2010. (In addition to helping connect us with *Delivering Happiness* fans online, Amy Jo also gave me invaluable snipe hunting lessons near Mt. Rushmore in South Dakota.)

Now, after three years of working together, we've decided to partner together in a much bigger way: by investing in Digital Royalty through VegasTechFund, the technology and start-up investment arm of our $350 million Downtown Project to help revitalize downtown Las Vegas.

One of our goals is to help transform downtown Las Vegas into the most community-focused large city in the world. We want to help inspire and empower people to follow their passions to create a vibrant, connected urban core. We are focused on accelerating community, accelerating serendipity, and accelerating learning.

I've witnessed Digital Royalty's growth over the past several years and am excited about the potential of Digital Royalty University. We are always interested in improving how people learn and are excited about its prospects for growth and contribution to community, serendipity, and learning.

When I first met Amy Jo several years ago, I asked her: "Why? Why are you doing what you're doing? Why do you want your company to get bigger?"

Over time, I've seen her shift her mind-set and business model to be more aligned with the answer to that question to fit her higher purpose in business and life.

Amy Jo has made her mark over the past three years with her digital media agency, Digital Royalty. With this book, *Renegades Write the Rules,* you'll learn about her unique story and perspective that can have an impact on your own approach to business and life as well.

Tony Hsieh
CEO, Zappos.com

More praise for *Renegades Write the Rules*

"Like people who say that they were in the crowd to watch Secretariat win the Belmont, so many people claim to have been an early adopter of social media. Amy Jo Martin is the genuine article. She was there from the beginning and has seen it all. Don't buy this book at your own peril."

—Darren Rovell (@DarrenRovell),
sports business reporter, ESPN

"*Renegades Write the Rules* is an engaging, well-written piece and an honest look at not just social media but the spirit of adventure and the benefits of risk-taking if you are willing to learn from your mistakes! Amy Jo writes with clarity and humor and provides the answers to the issues of social media. It's a fun read and full of priceless information for this digital age. As my father, Bruce Lee, would suggest, 'Use no way as way and have no limitation as limitation.' Amy Jo does just that! She is a true innovator and teacher."

—Shannon Lee (@BruceLeeLegacy),
CEO of Bruce Lee Enterprises

"Don't be fooled. *Renegades Write the Rules* may be the perfect social media tutorial, but Amy Jo's quest is much larger than just deconstructing Twitter or Facebook. She has led the way in teaching us all how to use the latest communication channels to turn branding and marketing on their heads. No longer do organizations, advertisers, or companies define the rules of the game; power now resides with the individual, the customer, the purchaser, or the fan. It's an entirely new ball game and *Renegades Write the Rules* explains why we all need to think differently in order to win."

—Scott Reifert (@WhiteSox),
senior vice president of communications, Chicago White Sox

"Thanks to *Renegades Write the Rules*, we all have a road map to guide us in the process of redefining our own personal and professional brands. With this book, Amy Jo has armed us with her core Renegade Rules, which if applied will help us achieve success within the social space. This book isn't just for athletes, celebrities, or brands. It's for everyone."

—Baron Davis (@Baron_Davis),
Believer and NBA Player

RENEGADES
WRITE
THE RULES

RENEGADES WRITE THE RULES

How the Digital Royalty Use Social Media to Innovate

Amy Jo Martin

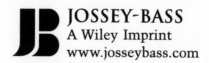

JOSSEY-BASS
A Wiley Imprint
www.josseybass.com

Published by Jossey-Bass
A Wiley Imprint
989 Market Street, San Francisco, CA 94103-1741—www.josseybass.com
Author is represented by literary agent Kevin Small of ResultSource.com.

Jossey-Bass books and products are available through most bookstores. To contact Jossey-Bass directly call our Customer Care Department within the U.S. at 800-956-7739, outside the U.S. at 317-572-3986, or fax 317-572-4002.

Wiley also publishes its books in a variety of electronic formats and by print-on-demand. Not all content that is available in standard print versions of this book may appear or be packaged in all book formats. If you have purchased a version of this book that did not include media that is referenced by or accompanies a standard print version, you may request this media by visiting http://booksupport.wiley.com. For more information about Wiley products, visit us www.wiley.com.

Library of Congress catalogue-in-publication data has been applied for.

ISBN: 978-1-118-34051-6 (print); ISBN: 978-1-118-44224-1 (ebk),
ISBN: 978-1-118-44228-9 (ebk), ISBN: 978-1-118-44230-2 (ebk)

Printed in the United States of America

FIRST EDITION
HB Printing   10 9 8 7 6 5 4 3 2 1

RENEGADES
WRITE
THE RULES

0

The Renegade Way

My hand had been slapped before. I was the director of digital media and research for the Phoenix Suns, a first-of-its-kind position within the National Basketball Association that I convinced leadership to let me launch. The position held one clear caveat: I was not to help the players with their personal brands or give them "Twitter tutorials."

The players didn't get that memo. They were asking for social media advice with increasing frequency, as was the league office.

For months, the Suns' weekly revenue meetings gained healthy tension when it came time for my report. I would inhale big and then spill my ideas on how to monetize this brave new world with the team's president, general manager, and senior vice presidents. I then put on my renegade hat and brought the social media full court press.

There were no rules at the time (it was 2008), and social media was the wild, wild west. My work and I represented risk and volatility to an otherwise conventional operation. I'd suggest "a tweet-up," and they'd say, "A what-up?" What I called opportunity they called naiveté. The tension eventually came to a head one afternoon on the team plane.

We were preparing to take off for Los Angeles for a game against the Lakers, and I was sitting in a window seat with my boss next to me. That's when I received a text from Shaquille O'Neal, who was sitting about ten rows up. He wanted some help setting up his Twitter account on his Shaqberry phone—his fifth in two months. I tried to ignore his request, ducking down nonchalantly to avoid self-incrimination. Again.

Shaquille is persistent.

When I didn't answer, he turned around and guided a "get your butt up here" wave directly at me. Nothing a seven-foot man does goes unnoticed. I gathered myself, stepped casually over my boss, and strolled to the front of the plane—nothing to see here.

Shaquille had accidentally locked his new phone and forgotten his password. He had just completed his ninth unlock attempt and had received a notification that he was on his final attempt. With big worried eyes, he asked if I knew his password.

I rattled off the last seven we had used for his social media accounts. This sparked his memory, and he unlocked the phone. It was a bittersweet victory.

Shaquille stood up, which is very up, gave me a high-five, and belted, "YOU'RE A GENIUS!"

I could feel myself blushing.

After a brief celebration dance, he proceeded to tell his Twitter followers—about 100,000 at the time—the same thing:

SHAQ
@SHAQ

I made a mistake @Phoenixsunsgirl, is a genius, I know she made a 1580 on her SAT

↩ Reply   ⇄ Retweet   ★ Favorite

25 Feb 09 via web

He then sat back down and began pitching me to two-time NBA Most Valuable Player Steve Nash as the queen of Twitter who would take his brand to the next level. No pressure.

I had already crossed the line by going up there to do the forbidden social media stuff, but this was the point of no return. I slinked back to my row with my eyes down, stepped over my boss, sank into my seat, and busied myself with something (anything!) on my laptop. I slowly swiveled toward the window and didn't look around for a while.

Despite the sweaty palms, the episode turned out to be a welcome nudge in the right direction.

The world of communication was rapidly changing with every new Facebook user, Twitter handle, and YouTube video. I was standing at the edge of the new world, and I could see the open frontier in front of me. I had a choice to make: stay in the cozy corporate gig or forge a path through the largely unknown expanse of social media.

When I thought about it, I realized I had already placed myself at odds with the norms of corporate protocol. I frequented the empty sports arena of the US Airways Center during work hours and set a makeshift work space away from my coworkers who weren't believers. I would do my work and escape the environment of healthy tension. When I was with them, I took their verbal jabs, wry grins, and knowing nods. I had blurred the lines between my traditional job responsibilities and what I knew needed to be done in order to innovate the way things were done. Change typically doesn't sit well with others. The truth was that I'd already developed the thick, weathered skin that comes from forging a path against the winds of "what we've always done."

The day after the plane incident, my boss called me a renegade. I told her I preferred to think of my approach as "coloring outside the lines without crossing the line." I then confessed I wanted to be free to design my own day and conquer new things.

Reflecting back, that first fearless step into the unknown was one of the most valuable steps I've ever taken. Recognizing and owning that feeling of daunting-yet-promising opportunity ahead would later become priceless.

I didn't have a grand plan, but I did have some basic inspiration. Just after labeling me a renegade, which I secretly enjoyed, my boss slid a piece of paper across her desk. On it she'd written three words:

Work. Family. Self.

"Choose two," she said. "You can't have all three."

It didn't sit right with me.

My boss proceeded to explain that she'd tried it and all three wasn't possible. If you wanted to be really good, she insisted, you had to choose two.

The antithesis of that philosophy immediately became a personal challenge. A few weeks later, I gave her my notice and then set out to have all three in abundance.

My vehicle? A first-of-its-kind social media consultancy I named Digital Royalty.

4

The rules? I would write them as I went.

What I've since discovered is that these new and spontaneously written rules of social media have forever changed the scope of innovation. I wasn't the only pioneer out there, but let's just say the landscape looked more like the wild, wild west than Woodstock back in the summer of 1969. Yet for the handful of us willing to brave the elements, the spoils of the land were abundant if we were willing to make mistakes early and learn on the fly. By the time we were building social media cities, late adopters were just beginning to make the mistakes we'd learned from years before.

The good news is that even if you're late in joining the new frontier called social media, you no longer have to stumble your way through a cracked and dry land to find water. A path has been forged that you can follow. I'm not saying you won't have to get on your boots and saddle up. You will have to break a sweat and wipe a bit of dust from your eyes. But this can be the ride of your life if you know where you're going.

I believe in the power of sharing battle stories. Some call them case studies, but those tend to slant things in favor of the case one is trying to prove. I prefer good old story time with the pretty and not-so-pretty details that better prepare the next brave soul to take a similar path. For this reason, I've collected personal innovation stories (and their subsequent lessons) from all types of renegades, from NBA Most Valuable Player Steve Nash, to DoubleTree by Hilton global head Rob Palleschi, to ESPN personality Darren Rovell and Bruce Lee's daughter, Shannon Lee, among many others. I'll also share some of my own lessons. I believe if we share stories that allow other people to leapfrog our mistakes and snag our lessons, we can accelerate the process of learning and thus of innovation.

This is a book about social media. It will usher you into the engine room of some of the world's most popular celebrities, strongest brands, and biggest sports icons with whom I have the honor of working. There you'll get an insider's look at how these culture shapers make social media work. I'll give you a clue: they don't just sign up for an account and ask for a shout-out. Their behind-the-scenes stories provide justification, inspiration, and prescription for making social media work in your own endeavors, whether you're starting from scratch or already running a multibillion-dollar operation.

This is also a book about innovation. It has to be. Innovation is being redefined by one primary force today: social media. It is irrational, even irresponsible, to start a business, launch a product, raise awareness, or build a brand today without including a social media strategy.

Consider the basic definition of *innovation*: "the creation of better or more effective products, processes, technology, services, and ideas that are accepted by markets, governments, and societies."[1] Now consider that Facebook and Twitter alone give any person on the planet access to more than 1 billion people—roughly 15 percent of the human race. No other medium in the history of humankind has that kind of reach. The latest Super Bowl set a new record for the most watched television show in history, with 111 million viewers. By comparison, that's only one-tenth the reach of the two-headed social media giant. Also, keep in mind that the Super Bowl is a once-a-year event. Social media is 24/7/365. Tapping just a fraction of its audience can give you a tremendous competitive advantage. Not to mention, it's a heck of lot cheaper than a sixty-second Super Bowl spot.

Ongoing engagement is no small benefit. Once it's established, success depends largely on your ability to keep the conversation going by asking the right questions, listening for the most common answers, and then innovating your business or brand accordingly. How? Deliver value when, where, and how your audience wants it. It's not much more complicated than that. Where I've found most people need help is coming up with creative ways to deliver this desired value. I happen to have some ideas, which I share in this book.

Consider collaboration, for instance. Facebook and Twitter alone often help you innovate "better or more effective products, processes, technology, services, and ideas" more effectively than any traditional poll, survey, or creative meeting. The rapid speed and giant scope of today's collaboration media have raised the bar for innovation. Anyone can inspire, initiate, test, and spread ideas like never before.

Take "Kony 2012," the thirty-minute video that took the world by storm in March 2012 and was viewed by more than 80 million people within two weeks. For a quarter of a century, Joseph Kony had terrorized the people of four African countries in relative anonymity. In less than two weeks, through an innovative online video, he became the most infamous man on the planet. Opinions of the video's producers aside, bringing the brutal Ugandan warlord to justice gained instantaneous, international attention that got people moving. The U.S. government took action. The countries of the African Union took action. And millions of citizens from countries around the globe took action, including celebrities like Oprah, Justin Bieber, and Kim Kardashian.

Sure, the film's success was about raising awareness for a cause. But you better believe that skillful, renegade-style marketing had a lot to do with that success. "Is there an Oscar for this sort of direction?" asked Bono of the video. "[The director] Jason Russell deserves it."[2]

Makes one rethink that $4 million Super Bowl ad budget. If not, it should.

Market research, consumer demand, customer satisfaction, and *brand reach*: these traditional marketing phrases have new life in a digital world. That's primarily because the idea of collaboration has exploded.

Traditional marketing and branding focus on telling customers what they need. There is little need for front-end communication with your target audience. Most, if not all, collaboration takes place after the transaction in the form of exit surveys and customer service conversations. The primary question collaboration answers is, "Did the product, service, and/or process meet your expectations?"

Today, however, audiences own the market and dictate the expectations (at least for a season—more on that later). The tool they offer is crowdsourcing.

It points to the crowd as the key resource, which it is. The funny thing is that this resource isn't new. You've always had the option to tap into the minds of your desired audience. It's just never before been this easy, effective, or profitable. And yet there are still plenty of skeptics. This book is for them too. My mission in this book is to win over all of you skeptics.

In each chapter, I address the common concerns I have come across as I take this renegade message into traditional branding meetings and classic corporate boardrooms. I call the most common concerns *innovation allergies*. For now, suffice it to say that the renegade way requires a new mind-set that unnerves traditional thinkers. Today's renegade way requires everyone to lose some control in order to achieve greater clarity. This is a core tenet of all effective social media strategies.

Clarity about what?

Generally, clarity about the direction your business is headed in. Is your business creating the right products? Is your idea worth $1 million or 1 million pesos? Is that brand of yours as memorable as the agency said it would be? Do people really care to hear about what kind of sushi you ate last night? They might.

To be more specific, I am talking about clarity of purpose. Are we just a shoe company—or something more? Do I really care about this product, or is it just a gimmick to turn heads and make a buck? Do I really want to go down in history as the vanilla villain or the king of cliché? I hope not, unless you're a really good comedian.

All of these questions can be answered succinctly if you're willing to loosen your grip on your current notions of reality. Wouldn't you rather know the truth about yourself, your brand, and your business future than continue living in Wonderland?

"Curiouser and Curiouser!" said Alice.[3] That's how we have to remain about ourselves, our brands, and our business ventures in general. And the answers to our curiosities are often out there to be discovered. Innovation is never static. Now we have a place to keep it dynamic.

I'll be the first to admit I like being in control. This comes as no surprise to anyone who knows me. It's one of the main reasons I continued helping the Suns players with their social media accounts despite warnings from the brass. I knew there was untapped potential for the franchise in the players' personal brands.

Maintaining control is also the reason I eventually quit my job with the Suns. There was a future to jump into that couldn't wait for corporate approval. Today, being in control is one of the main reasons my workweeks look more like an *Amazing Race* episode than one from *The Office*. Control can be a very good thing.

It can also limit your potential. Things get stodgy if you are the only voice worth listening to—whether you are a Fortune 100 executive, an iconic celebrity, or a stifled entrepreneur surrounded by four carpeted walls. Yes, being a renegade absolutely requires individuality and ownership. It also requires a fearless ability to toss your ideas and philosophies, methods, and products into a body of water that might contain piranhas.

It's often your only way of reaching the promised land. No matter how sharp or seasoned you are, this intentional loss of control is a main component of pioneering today because it's the quickest and most effective way to measure the value of just about anything you do.

When my Suns boss slid that piece of paper across her desk, it represented a philosophy many nine-to-fivers have accepted as truth: you simply can't have it all. Something's gotta give: work, family, or self. I didn't buy it, and neither should you. But I didn't have proof when I ventured out on my own. My counterphilosophy had to be tested. And so did my business plan.

What better than to test both with the people with whom I already had a history? At the least, I knew they'd tell me the truth. I could have been dead wrong about either, and it would have cost me a promising career with a stable organization. But risk is unavoidable along the renegade path.

As it turned out, I wasn't dead wrong, and the cost to me would have been far greater had I not given up some control and tested a better way and a new business.

The reason the (ad)venture worked—and continues to work—is that I chose to employ the crowd interdependently. This is another core tenet to making social media work. I independently developed my philosophy and my business idea, and then I depended on the crowd for feedback. I knew they would either prove me right, almost right, or off my rocker. The way I saw it, I had a 66 percent chance of succeeding as long as I didn't dismiss the crowd. So I stuck my neck out and then listened to see if I'd survive.

Could someone have it all, and if so, what were the best ways? Was there a market for a social media consultancy, and if so, what might it look like?

I had my notions, which I always controlled, but I also let go of the belief that my notions were spot on. I floated my ideas into the crowd because I knew the best idea might be a combination of my spark of innovation and others fanning the flame.

Before social media, the world primarily used the crowd (target market, voting bloc, Super Bowl viewership) either dependently to get validation or independently to sell the crowd something they thought the crowd needed. Now you don't have to guess. People are more than willing to tell you what they want, need, and think. It's the renegade's best resource.

But you have to be careful.

I'm not suggesting your brand or business should become a piece of driftwood that's tossed to and fro in the waves of others' opinions. There's little stability in that. I'm suggesting that today's best entrepreneurs, businesses, and brands don't keep their ships in the harbor. They venture out with a direction in mind but also with an understanding that the wind and waves might teach them a lesson or two. Ventures should equal adventures, after all.

What makes people renegades is their ability to stick with what is sticking, despite the occasional criticism, wry grins, and knowing nods. Egos take a back seat because the renegade must often digest the positive feedback with the useful critique in order to make the best course corrections. The original idea played out to the tilt? The original idea slightly upgraded? A new idea altogether?

When I set out on my own, I knew two things: (1) my intent was pure (I wanted to design my own day and help businesses and brands become more influential by connecting with their audiences) and (2) I had an idea to start a social media consultancy in order to do it. All innovation begins there, with intent and an idea.

Despite the strategic interdependence required today, it would be wrong to say today's renegades are not original thinkers. "Two heads are better than one" is often quoted but very misleading.[4]

"Nothing was ever created by two men," wrote John Steinbeck. "Once the miracle of creation has taken place, the group can build and extend it, but the group never invents anything. The preciousness lies in the lonely mind of a man."[5]

Alex Osborn was a founding partner of the famous advertising agency BBDO. He's also the guy credited with coining a term so popular it still spills from our mouths on a weekly basis, especially in business settings. In Chapter 33 of his 1953 best-seller, *Applied Imagination*, Osborn suggested that when a group works together, the members should engage in a "brainstorm."[6]

Oh, how we love the brainstorm.

Got a client problem? Brainstorm the solution. Need a great product idea? Brainstorm some ideas. Want a new logo? Let's brainstorm!

The trouble is, brainstorming doesn't work the way we think it does. Ultimately the original idea is still the sole necessary root.

In his January 30, 2012, *New Yorker* article, journalist Jonah Lehrer reminds us that "the first empirical test of Osborn's brainstorming technique was performed at Yale University, in 1958. The results were a sobering refutation of Osborn. Although the findings did nothing to dent brainstorming's popularity, numerous follow-up studies have come to the same conclusion."[7]

Lehrer points out the problem: brainstorming's most important component, according to Osborn, is the absence of criticism and negative feedback. "Creativity is so delicate a flower," Osborn insisted, "that praise tends to make it bloom while discouragement often nips it in the bud."

Really?

Innovation has always required thick skin—perhaps more so today with the tidal waves of commentary that always seem to follow big ideas (à la "Kony 2012" or Obamacare)—but if a few discouraging comments derail you, you may be better off staying inside those cubicle walls. Trust me, they will surface.

The truth is that debate and critical feedback have been repeatedly proven to bring out our best. And that's a big benefit of social media, not brainstorming. Today's renegades thrive off both positive and negative feedback because together they paint the clearest picture of reality, whether that's the street perception of your brand, the practicality of your product, or the comprehension of your core message. With social media, this clarifying information is at your fingertips 24/7 if you're willing to seek it out. Renegades lead a charge, take the high-fives and repetitive hand slaps in stride, and continue moving.

In the second half of his article, Jonah Lehrer describes what has been proven time and again to be the ultimate environment for creative breakthrough: "a space with an almost uncanny ability to extract the best from people . . . a magical incubator."

Yes, renegades are initiators. But it is also important to see that through social media, they boldly provide that magical incubator for their ideas. Sometimes those original ideas stick from square one. Sometimes they morph into bigger and better ideas that can move masses.

Why would you risk your precious IP to the crowd? Because you believe a better idea might surface after the initial splash. And because you ultimately know that a bigger body of water creates a stronger wave of momentum.

> Renegades know that their team is their best asset. My friend Lucy Danziger, Editor-in-Chief of *SELF Magazine,* once told me that her secret to success was hiring only people who are smarter than she is. Everyone who works for Lucy knows it's his or her number one duty to teach her and one another. It's their job to show up, work hard, teach, and learn. Intuitively, I've always understood this concept, but referring to it as "hiring a team of teachers" brought it home for me and offers a refreshing new slant to company culture.

It takes a certain kind of stubbornness to be a renegade. You do what needs to be done—even if the formula doesn't yet exist. Fortunately this is an inclination I've had since I was a kid (but things netted out just fine, don't you think, Mom and Dad!).

When I turned sixteen and my sexy, chrome-rimmed Mercury Cougar got its first flat in the Walmart parking lot, I called my dad. When he arrived and proceeded to retrieve the iron, jack, and spare, I stopped him in his tracks. I let him know I would be changing the tire. He could just tell me what to do.

Had I ever changed a tire before? Nope. Did I have any idea what I was doing? I'd seen movies. The point is that I wanted to learn, and I knew the quickest way was to just go for it and absorb the lessons along the way.

13

Enlisting social media might feel like changing your first flat tire at sixteen. This book will serve as your how-to manual. But you won't have to do it alone. I will serve as the practiced onlooker who's changed a few tires in my day, including my own.

When I was still with the Suns, my secret, mad scientist experiments eventually turned into best practices, but not in that setting. I kept hearing our marketing partners (sponsors such as Coke and Verizon Wireless) say that they wanted to get closer to fans and athletes. No longer were our marketing partners as interested in venue signage or TV spots. I started listening to Suns fans using social media and joined in their conversation. I stayed up late and responded to everyone. I made friends I still have today. I invested in my relationships and showed people the Suns cared about what they thought. And I learned what they wanted.

The problem was that I couldn't fully deliver on their desires in my current position. I had a flat tire in the Phoenix Suns parking lot. At twenty-nine years old, I knew I needed a change. This time my dad was standing by me only in spirit. The hard work I had to figure out on my own.

On one hand, I have. My clients range from the presidents and CEOs of brands everyone knows to the professional athletes and celebrities millions love. On the other hand, I am still learning on the fly. That's the nature of social media and innovation. Sometimes renegades wing it. While some of the landscape has come into focus, it is still ever changing, still a frontier to be discovered. There are rules that have clearly been defined, but there are also new rules to be written.

One of the best perks of being an entrepreneur is the ability to design your own day. Whether it's taking conference calls during a mountain-top hike or working on the manuscript for this very book while getting a pedicure, I've found that I am most creative outside the office, when I'm not sitting in front of a desk. Yet one of the healthiest challenges about owning your own company is the fact that "work" never stops—especially when your business revolves around social media. It's up to you to break that routine and go to a place that inspires you to do your best work. We spend a majority of our waking hours at our jobs. Given that we get only one shot at life, shouldn't we be enjoying ourselves every minute possible? Why not change the way we think? As Tony Hsieh, CEO of Zappos, has been known to say, cheers to work/life integration versus separation. Another perk of social media.

A few months ago, we wouldn't have imagined that a thirty-minute video could possibly captivate 80 million people in less than two weeks. Now we know it's possible. There's a lesson to be learned. There will continue to be lessons to learn.

The renegade way is an unquenchable spirit of innovation that often springs from an unquenchable thirst for learning.

In the pages to come, I cover what has been learned about social media to this point and the subsequent rules that define the current landscape. Apply these rules to make social media work for you. But always remain curious. No one has discovered the full potential of social media yet.

In this context, a virtually unknown brand can quickly become well known. An old business model can quickly be revolutionized. And here's the kicker: this doesn't just translate to virtual traffic. It translates to real dollars.

No longer is social media a fad. Today it's a frontline strategy for any business or brand wanting monetizable exposure and, more important, a highly lucrative, low-cost way to connect and stay connected to target audiences. Despite what some say, there is a quantifiable return on social media. You might be on the fence right now, but by the time we're done, you'll be in the renegade camp.

Some brands are already employing the renegade rules we're about to discuss, and I applaud them. They embrace all forms of innovation, especially through social media. I'll introduce you to several of them and to others in their same industries who don't yet get it—and if they don't get it soon, they will fade further back in the competitive landscape.

If you're part of a renegade company, use your freedom to explore. This is often where the best lessons are learned and where you can add the most bang for your positional buck. You'll find lots more inspiration in the examples I cover.

If, in contrast, you find yourself stuck due to your company's outdated mind-set or because you are too unsure of your skills, don't worry. I'll stand by and show you how to proceed from that first crank of the car jack. Your job is to just go for it and learn along the way. You'll be cruising in no time.

Whoever coined the term *social media* didn't do us any favors. It's not media, it was not invented for marketers and advertisers, and people don't welcome it. They welcome conversation and value exchange. These progressive new communication channels are more like the telephone than the television. People often ask me, "How do you monetize social media?" I reply, "How are you monetizing your telephone?" Communicating with your consumers, fans, or guests is a core function of business. Doing it well is a common difference between mediocre brands and memorable ones. Not having a strong, two-way communication strategy is like not unlocking your doors for business or answering the phone when customers call. If you would never do those things, you should never ignore social communication channels or, shall we say, social media.

When I was a kid, my family moved five times before I was in the sixth grade. At first, it was disconcerting. Saying good-bye to people and things I'd grown accustomed to wasn't easy. Then at some point, it wasn't so hard. I came to accept that change is necessary because it is the only way anything remains exciting and new.

Today social media represents the greatest, most necessary change in the business landscape. You can resist this change, but you can't stop it. Or you can embrace what's new and become a renegade who helps frame the new rules of marketing, branding, and innovation in general. As you're about to see, the rules aren't rocket science, but they take guts and ingenuity. I can promise you the ride is always new and exciting. Are you in? Tweet me @AmyJoMartin with the #TeamRenegades hashtag to let me know you're with me.

RULE 1

Be the Media

Innovation Allergy: *Lack of Skill*

Just three years after the Suns' "plane incident," I was standing in a home office where a fifteen-second Tout video tweet launched an unprecedented firestorm of media activity. The time was 3:01 P.M. The date was June 1, 2011. By 3:05, the subject of the video was the number one worldwide trending topic on Twitter, a list derived from more than 250 million messages by 250 million users per day. By 3:15, a major media outlet had picked up the video and replayed it during a broadcast in progress. Thousands of other outlets immediately followed suit. The story was global in less than fifteen minutes, and the swell of interest mounted in the hours and days that followed.

All this from a strategically placed tweet?

You bet.

The video's author?

NBA superstar Shaquille O'Neal.

The video's message?

His retirement announcement after a storied nineteen-year career:

SHAQ
@SHAQ

im retiring Video: http://bit.ly/kvLtE3
#ShaqRetires

↩ Reply   🔁 Retweet   ★ Favorite

1 Jun via web

While Shaquille's message was brief, it instantly engaged his 3.9 million Twitter followers and 2.1 million Facebook fans, triggering a ripple effect that would have been unthinkable just a few months earlier. Beyond the initial 201,255 video views, Shaquille's Facebook page received more than 620,000 impressions (an impression is an estimate of the number of people a particular piece of content reaches), 4,400 visitor comments, and 30,000 new "likes" in less than one day. In the same time frame, he added more than 60,000 new Twitter followers, and Google searches for his name increased by nearly 1,600 percent.

It would be naive to call this sort of attention normal for anyone using social media. So that's not the point here. Shaquille is an NBA legend, and his announcement signified the end of an era. Yet it would also be a mistake to dismiss it as an anomaly and conclude that social media is not worth your time.

The mind-boggling statistics of Shaquille's tweet are ultimately the result of a creative, personalized communication strategy that anyone can use as a template for social media success and much more. The foundation is an understanding of a major shift that has occurred in our media-driven world that established a new rule of innovation.

20

SportsBiz with Darren Rovell: Shaq's Retirement Gives Big Boost to New Company

Forbes: How Shaq Put Tout on the Social Media Map (in 15 Seconds)

ESPN Sportscenter: All-Access: Behind Shaq's Social Media Retirement Blitz

No longer do the broadcasters, advertisers, and PR moguls control the news. In the digital age, *you* are the media.

If the 2011 revolution in Egypt revealed anything, it showed us that we are hyperconnected people who swarm around what matters most at that moment. What matters can come from anywhere at any moment because the foundation of social media success is not Nielsen ratings. The foundation is mattering in the moments of people's lives. The more often you matter, the more often people will tune in. How, then, do you matter?

That's the key question, whether you're a celebrity wanting to raise awareness or promote a show, or an entrepreneur wanting to win more business or solicit more feedback.

The answer is simple: to matter, you have to continually deliver something your audience finds valuable, even if that value is simply great entertainment. The main difference today is that you don't have to fight to deliver value during a prime-time slot on a major network. You just have to hit Post, Update, or Send.

How do you know what your audience values?

That's also simple: use social media to listen, and then continue the dialogue.

Turning On Your Channel

When I gave my notice with the Suns, Shaquille became my first client. The truth is that when he and I initially set sail into the unchartered waters of social media, we didn't have a hard and fast plan. We simply had the nerve to try just about anything to discover what worked. Shaquille was just as much a renegade as I was. I didn't have to talk him into doing anything. He was a gamer even when he didn't fully understand the game.

While I was still with the Suns, he and I had quietly managed to build his following to approximately 100,000 on the back of his NBA popularity. Still, we knew that his following represented only a fraction of the audience he could have. We also knew his influence was limited at best. His followers were largely voyeurs hoping to get glimpses of a superstar's lifestyle, which may have been a disappointment since Shaquille doesn't act like a typical superstar. In addition, there were some doubters who thought all the tweets were coming from me, Shaqeteering as his ghost tweeter. We needed to prove it was Shaquille behind it all because if it wasn't really him, the communication just wasn't as interesting.

I knew he had this huge persona people had come to know primarily through TV ads, billboards, and legendary dunks. That guy was "Shaq," and he was a good place to start. But my goal was to help people get to know the Shaquille behind the Shaq.

Shaquille is the big guy who is more than the billboard and backboard-breaking persona. He has clumsy thumbs and changes (a nicer word than *loses*) phones nearly as much as he changes clothes. He also has zero ability to fake anything and loves more than anything to make people laugh. He was the perfect social media guinea pig.

I sensed that if people could get to know the real Shaquille behind the Shaq persona, we'd have an online brand people could relate to and enjoy. If it could be done, this was our best shot at scaling the Shaq brand.

The big question was how to bottle up his huge personality and bring it down home in the social space. There wasn't yet a precedent in the sports world, so we relied primarily on intuition and humor, which tend to go over better than a mission statement and a customer pledge.

Shaquille's fans from Phoenix, Cleveland, and Boston all became accustomed to a social media concept I developed and coined "Random Acts of Shaqness." Whether we were driving foot traffic to a marketing partner's store

with our "hide and tweet" stunts (where we'd hide something of value and tweet its whereabouts, like the game of hide and seek), increasing awareness about an event, or promoting a new product, Shaquille's random acts would encourage followers in a particular city to search for hidden prizes on their streets, like autographed jerseys or upcoming event tickets. He would even invite his Twitter followers to have lunch with him and give them a personal phone call. The key to its success was a continual stream of deeper engagement matched with a pure intent.

For fans to get each clue from Shaquille, they had to remain by their phones. In the early days, we might have two dozen fans participating. That number quickly rose to the hundreds and then thousands as word spread and fans from cities we hadn't considered began requesting we bring the game there. So we did.

Shaquille once hid an autographed *Sports Illustrated* at the West Side Market in Cleveland and tweeted its location to more than 2.5 million followers.

It took a fan five minutes to find the signed copy and thirty minutes for local media to cover the story.

In another Random Act of Shaqness, Shaquille told a Twitter follower he was going to call her. Disbelieving, she played along and sent her cell number in a direct message (DM). Two minutes later, she received a call. She nearly passed out when she heard Shaquille's deep voice on the other end. What made this have an impact on a large scale was our ability to hypersyndicate the live video and photos back to Shaquille's fans and followers in real time. If you were in China, Canada, or Australia, you could keep up with the play-by-play because we repurposed the live content right back to the larger audience of millions, who loved following along.

One of the all-time fan favorites was when Shaquille, who had just days before being traded from Cleveland to Boston, tweeted that he would be heading to Harvard Square in twenty minutes. It was important to him to blend into his new community.

SHAQ
@SHAQ

I mean on my way to harvard square lol dam I phone my fingers r to big statue time

↩ Reply   ⇄ Retweet   ★ Favorite

about 22 hours ago via TweetDeck
Retweeted by 100+ people

He showed up right on time, took a seat on a park bench, and played a statue for nearly an hour while fans posed with him for pictures. The media showed up to cover the stunt, and the crowd swelled so big that the police had to step in. (Yes, he looked pretty much like this the entire time!)

These were never bait and switches, that is, cheap gimmicks to turn into transactions. They were genuine attempts to humanize the connection between Shaquille and his followers and discover what they really enjoyed. And we did them as often as we could.

When a social media endorsement deal came along, the first-ever for a sports star, we saw it as another opportunity to have some fun while going deeper with fans. The deal was for a health wellness brand, and Shaquille's role was simply to make his fans aware of the products. Like the renegades we are, we quickly decided to go all out.

Shaquille tweeted that he was going on the "Shaq-Lyte" diet and asked if any followers wanted to join him. We briefly mapped out the diet on Facebook, which we developed and endorsed, and then laid out the lone rule: "If you cheat you have to tweet." While we found creative ways for him to occasionally weave product promotion into his communication, we made the decision ahead of time to focus on the people, not the products.

Everyone knows diets are fun suckers, so allowing people to follow a seven-foot, 335-pound, malnourished athlete proved to be a smart and incredibly comical strategy. Thousands of fans joined the Shaq-Lyte craze and regularly engaged in conversations about it, primarily because everyone reveled in cheating.

They were not alone.

I don't recall how long Shaquille stayed on the diet, but suffice it to say it probably wasn't weeks with an "s." Before long he caved to his cravings, and to honor the single diet rule, he tweeted a photo of the incriminating evidence.

Even we didn't expect the effect it had.

Fans went berserk. In fact, it resonated so much that to this day, the ice cream tweet is still one of Shaquille's best all-time performing tweets—receiving more comments and retweets than even those with personal photos of him and LeBron James, Dwyane Wade, or Kobe Bryant.

The overwhelming response echoed a sentiment we'd already shared between us. The Shaq persona was fine for traditional marketing, but when it came to the avant-garde marketing of social media, nothing was more valuable to fans—and more viral—than Shaq being Shaquille. In fact, once millions got to know Shaquille, traditional efforts became that much more effective. He was suddenly more than an untouchable sports icon who only shattered backboards and did funny ads. He was someone people could relate to. He was even someone people could see themselves hanging out with.

His following began to steadily climb, as did other brands' awareness of Shaquille's marketing platform. Every week we came up with new and entertaining ways to bridge the virtual and physical worlds and ultimately boost fans one rung higher on the loyalty ladder. It was about this time that I had an epiphany. Social media was developing Shaquille O'Neal's brand in a way never before possible. Nonsports fans who didn't know anything about Shaquille, other than the fact that he was super tall, were now big fans of his. People from all over the world followed Shaquille because they were exposed to his personality day in and day out. He reached and recruited a much larger and diverse audience than his TV presence ever could.

As we continued blazing this path, what began as a voyeuristic following soon turned into a deeply devoted following. We knew we'd reached rare air when Oprah's team called and asked if Shaquille would tweet a response to her first official tweet. In a way only Shaquille could, he turned the opportunity into something that would make his followers laugh.

Oprah tweeted her message using full caps, effectively shouting her first tweet. Shaquille didn't miss a beat. His fans—and Oprah's—ate it up.

The exchange made it clear that Shaquille and his followers had established their own communication channel. If Harpo was calling on @THE_REAL_SHAQ to help broadcast @Oprah's news, there was no need to involve the press corps to broadcast Shaquille's news. I gave Shaquille a black belt in social media that day. He was connecting with fans one-to-one at the same time he was connecting with the millions. He had become the media—the new and improved media.

This is one of the new rules that has changed today's business and branding landscape. Social media, especially Twitter, democratize access. Traditional gatekeepers (editors, authority figures, governments) and physical boundaries

Oprah Winfrey
@Oprah

HI TWITTERS. THANK YOU FOR A WARM
WELCOME. FEELING REALLY 21ST CENTURY.

↩ Reply   ⇄ Retweet   ★ Favorite

about 1 hour ago from the web

SHAQ
@Shaq

@Oprah ur caps r on, btw

about 1 hour ago from the web

(especially distance) have lost their relevance to a global network where, if you deliver value, you and your ideas are granted global access.

Yes, renegades become the media. However, to build a loyal, lucrative following, you have to let your audience help you define what is newsworthy. Shaquille is a master at this, primarily because he is not so caught up in feeding his own ego that he can't hear what others are saying.

Taking the Me out of Media

The decision made for good ratings. It even raised more than $2 million for the Boys & Girls Clubs of America, and that's a great thing. But what was the residue left behind after LeBron James's one-hour ESPN special, hailed as "The Decision," when he announced he was leaving the Cleveland Cavaliers to join the Miami Heat? Maybe Dallas Mavericks' outspoken owner Mark Cuban summed it up best—if not understatedly so—when he told Dallas sports radio's *Dunham and Miller Show*, "I think he got bad advice."

While Cuban is not, as far as I know at least, privy to a branding algorithm that verifies the future value of a brand, his additional comment that James "lost a billion dollars in brand equity, give or take a couple bucks" made an important point. "The Decision" was ultimately an old-school PR stunt that controlled a message for the wrong reason.

The decision, the actual decision, was certainly LeBron's to make. But what would have been the effect if, instead of keeping everyone in the dark until the grandiose announcement, he engaged his fans in conversation about the decision? What if he had even asked for their opinions and then let the people who ultimately determine the value of his brand be privy to his decision before anyone else?

I'm not suggesting he should have taken a poll and moved wherever the majority of his followers told him to go. I'm merely suggesting—no, I'm actually stating—that the result of "The Decision" would have turned out quite differently if he'd taken the time to give his followers a little more access. Who knows? The majority may have sympathized with the choice he had to make. They may have even agreed on his ultimate choice.

Quite a different result from what actually happened. LeBron had promised his fans who had subscribed to his e-newsletters and followed his never-used-before Twitter account that they would be the first to hear "The Decision." In the end, it was quite a different brand valuation for arguably the NBA's best player.

As it stands, LeBron James's announcement serves as a stark contrast to Shaquille O'Neal's retirement announcement in effect and financial upshot. The primary difference was in the intent of the message. The intent behind the decisions we make has a dramatic impact on our level of influence and ability to innovate.

LeBron's message boomeranged back at him. The conversation between him and his audience was nonexistent. His communication was a self-promotional monologue. People were left to critique him since their closest connection to LeBron was hearing him talk about himself.

Shaquille's message pointed straight to his audience. When I arrived at his house in Orlando that June morning, he had already prerecorded a few retirement videos for me to review. He wanted this to be right, and so he had made a couple different options.

One was of him standing in front of pictures of former superstar teammates Kobe Bryant and Dwyane Wade, thanking them for the championships and all the good times on the court. It was interesting from a sports history standpoint but more Shaq than Shaquille. Another prerecording was Shaquille being the larger-than-life personality who loves to make people laugh. It was definitely him, but this was more than a typical, entertaining tweet. It was his retirement announcement after a Hall of Fame career. It required more of him.

I watched the videos over his shoulder and could tell he wasn't happy with either. We both knew they weren't right. Then I looked at him and said, "What do you really want to say to all your fans who've been with you all these years? What do you want to tell them now that you're retiring from the game you love?"

I could see him getting emotional. I grabbed his cell phone, opened the screen to shoot a new video, and handed it back to him. What came next is what the world watched just after 3:00 P.M. on June 1, 2011:

**We did it. Nineteen years baby. I want to thank you very much.
That's why I'm telling you first: I'm about to retire. Love you. Talk to
you soon.**

On that afternoon, this gigantic personality with a multimillion-dollar brand and arguably the most dominating presence in NBA history stepped out of his size 19 shoes once again to show his fans how important they were. By forgoing the flash bulbs and film reels of a traditional press conference and whispering his big announcement to their Twitter and Facebook accounts first, he become the first professional athlete to retire over social media.

Why did it work? Shaquille wasn't looking for anything in return. He truly cares for his followers, and the video was for them.

This is the paradox of becoming your own press corps: your messages will have their largest, most loyal reach when you take the "me" out of media. Shaquille understood from the beginning that social media is about the "social" more than the "media." The result? Today's largest sports networks now follow him to get the inside scoop.

Five minutes after retiring, he was back at it, asking followers for a new nickname to usher him into the next phase of his career. This nicknaming had also become something of an M.O.

The nicknames first began with Shaq, which soon changed to Superman due to Shaquille's obsession with the Man of Steel. Then came the Diesel and then his two acronyms: M.D.E. for Most Dominant Ever, which came after winning three straight NBA titles with the Lakers, and then L.C.L. for Last Center Left, a comical nod to his claim that he was the last true center in the NBA. Then there was Wilt Chamberneazy, a tribute to NBA legend Wilt Chamberlain. And then The Big Deporter, which Shaquille dubbed himself after eliminating Arvydas Sabonis and Rik Smits from the playoffs and sending both players back to their native countries for good. The Big Felon came after Shaquille made a game-winning steal against the Orlando Magic. The Big Sidekick was a self-deprecating name he took on after playing with superstar guards Kobe Bryant, Dwyane Wade, and LeBron James.

And of course when I was getting to know Shaquille, he was The Big Cactus, a name he took on after his trade to the Phoenix Suns.

Clearly his latest request for a new nickname was nothing new for his fans, who ramped up their engagement even more. Shaquille was right in the middle of the action.

The request was made at approximately 3:20 P.M. that retirement day, and at the time Shaquille hit tweet, we were still standing in his home office. Five minutes later, we had moved to his kitchen, where ESPN was on TV. I looked up and scrolling across the bottom of the screen was Shaquille's nickname request in quotes. The sportscaster then weaved the tweet into the broadcast, even parroting Shaquille's next tweet in near real time that claimed The Big 401K was currently in the lead with The Big Social Media Center, and the Big AARP running close behind (the Big AARP won).

From the Shaqberry, as we affectionately called his phones (even when he got an iPhone), to a major media broadcast in minutes—twice. Whoever says social media isn't relevant is way off base.

The truth is that social media is today's primary source of relevance. And you should be your prime-time channel.

RULE 2

Show Some Skin

Innovation Allergy: *Loss of Control*

Today's success rises and falls on human connection. But wait. Hasn't it always? Since the advent of the digital age or, truthfully, long before technology started taking over the world, we began to downplay the central role human connection plays in any business and branding endeavor. Instead of business being about affinity and intimacy, it came to be about persuasion and fulfillment. While there's nothing wrong with good old-fashioned salesmanship, when gimmicks and goods supplant handshakes and high fives, the ship has gone off course from the outset.

The trouble today is that even if we can agree that the advent of social media has swung the branding pendulum back toward the importance of human touch points, connection is easy to counterfeit. Or is it?

You can establish relationships in so many ways, but all have one overarching caveat: you can attempt to be whoever you want to be behind a laptop or smart phone screen. What's worse is that we live in an age that often rewards the veneered identities as much as the authentic ones—at least where popularity is concerned. So what's the upside to putting yourself out there, in real or fictitious fashion?

It's a good question, and one I'm asked often by business executives and entrepreneurs alike. My answer is always the same: people don't connect with logos and taglines; they connect with other people. So you have a choice: build a business that doesn't truly connect with its intended audience or build one that does.

At this point, there is usually some shifting in seats as I explain that the number one branding question today is not, "What is your brand?" but rather, "Who is your brand?" Most know what's coming next.

Who will be your brand's "who"?

Excuses are like _____ (you fill in the blank). We all have them, and if I haven't heard them all, I'd be surprised. Despite accepting that social media has advantages, despite agreeing that the president or CEO is the person in the best position to represent and influence a company's brand, and despite admitting that their business should have a "better social media presence," many top-flight executives and entrepreneurs still run from exposure.

NFL commissioner Roger Goodell is a good example. He built a following not really believing in social media, which is a nice way to say he was playing not to lose versus playing to win. He had people on his staff tweeting for him. There was little if any connection with his followers, who stuck around largely in hopes of getting a scrap of information from his poker-faced tweets.

Did anyone get to know the man behind the most popular sport in the United States? If they did, I don't know how. There was little personality beyond what anyone could muster from the scripted media clips and newspaper quotes. Then the looming 2010 lockout situation heated up, and Goodell's account went dark. He was completely missing for months, hiding in his Twitter closet. What he didn't consider is that Twitter closets have transparent doors. People knew he was in there statue-like and covering his mouth, like a kid who thinks closing his eyes equals invisibility.

What message did Goodell's sudden silence send? For starters, it confirmed that his following wasn't very important to him in the first place. He'd taken the stage, dimmed the lights, and then turned his back on the audience.

If you followed the noise on Twitter, you know the other immediate conclusion the world came to: he had something to hide. Whether or not he really did.

I realize the story is enough to scare some of you away from social media completely. "Aha!" you say. "That's exactly why I *WILL NEVER* embrace social media." Fair enough. But first consider this.

Was Goodell really better off staying away from social media in the first place, or did he just mishandle a golden opportunity to build trust and loyalty for his brand at a time when his audience was hanging on his every word?

If you're a renegade, you know the answer. And even if you're not, you probably know too.

Sure, Goodell could have avoided social media, remained untouchable to the general public, and continued laying down his laws and one-liners from on high. But what good does that do for the NFL? Ultimately it pits a man who is the face of its corporate brand against its owners, players, and raving fans who ultimately make the NFL a multibillion-dollar enterprise.

Is detachment from the top the way to grow the NFL brand? Not if the owners, players, and fans remain a critical part of its success.

This isn't a question of right or wrong as much as it's a question of good or great. Will the NFL brand go under because Goodell is a ghost on Twitter? No. The NFL brand is in good standing generally. It's the most popular sport in the United States with a signature event that is viewed by more people than any other event. But is the NFL prone to image problems? You bet it is. The quickest way to stay in front of problems and elevate the good traits of the brand is through social media. Here's why.

Traditional branding attempts to build loyalty through sponsorships and the placement and timing of logos and taglines. But does knowing a brand like, say, Pepsi is "the choice of a new generation," make us loyal to this fizzy brown beverage? That's a bit of a stretch. The people I know who drink Pepsi do so because they like the taste better than they do Coke. And if you want to compete on something as arbitrary as taste, that's your prerogative. Keep the traditional ads coming, and taste will remain fans' highest value regarding the Pepsi brand.

But I bet that's not the field Pepsi wants to live and die on. Judging by its growing social media presence, I'm pretty certain the powers that be want to stake fans' loyalty on something less finicky than taste buds. So should you.

Today, that "something" is at your fingertips. It begins with connections with fans that grow to a community bonded by common interest and common identity.

There is nothing more concrete in business than a relational connection. Among the many shifting preferences of your audience, their relational desires shift the least.

We all want to be seen and heard by others. We want to be valued for what we can offer others. We all want to belong to a community of others who value what we value—who are, in some important way, like us. What happens when a brand fulfills these wants? People stick around for more.

In contrast to traditional branding, social media focuses on building loyalty through community because, as we've already said, humans connect with humans, not logos. With this kind of connection expected, it's becoming more and more necessary for brands to introduce their personalities in some capacity because logos have zero ability to socialize.

The controlled messages of traditional branding are largely distrusted in a world where social media can quickly expose them as disingenuous or deceitful. Add to that the widely known option for any brand to go deeper than "the choice of a new generation," and your brand is faced with looking snooty, outdated, or simply aloof if you don't take the plunge.

Going deeper, putting your brand's personality out there by revealing the person or people behind the product or logo, builds trust. Affinity is the first step to building trust, which is the first step to increasing loyalty. If your brand employs a person who embodies at least one human trait your fans find valuable, that person and your fans need to meet and get to know one another.

This human connection to brands isn't groundbreaking. If you think about your favorite brands, you'll typically be able to identify the people you connect with, whether it's a CEO you heard speak, a celebrity who endorses the brand, or someone you know directly who works for or advocates for the brand.

There's usually a human touch point that makes that brand more meaningful to you than your agreement with a tagline.

If the president of your company, the most influential person behind your brand, hasn't attempted to make that connection, then he or she is missing a major opportunity not only to build trust and increase loyalty but also to avoid looking aloof. There is also money left on the table.

Today's top celebrities, businesses, and sports icons know that the quickest way to monetize their brands is to humanize them. To the chagrin of inaccessible executives everywhere, there is no way to humanize anything without some level of exposure. Don't worry—you don't have to let it all hang out. But you do have to show some skin to prove your humanity. Here's the kicker: humans make mistakes, so get used to it.

In contrast to the NFL's top man, another global sports organization wasted no time worrying about exposure. As a result, this organization has taken a growth trajectory unheralded in the history of sports, to the point that many have declared it the world's fastest-growing sport over the past five years.

Since purchasing the Ultimate Fighting Championship a decade ago, brothers Frank and Lorenzo Fertitta, along with Dana White, have kept the sport of mixed martial arts (MMA) at the forefront of innovation, forging new paths with fans and sponsors where paths did not exist. Today the UFC produces more than thirty live events worldwide each year, and it boasts the most successful and longest-running sports reality show in history, *The Ultimate Fighter*. UFC programming is available in over 354 million homes in more than 145 countries, in 19 languages. The UFC also holds the distinction as the largest live pay-per-view event provider in the world.

The explosive growth of the UFC brand is no fluke. It's primary engine for growth? Major social media exposure that gives fans real-time connections with not only the individual fighters but also one of its founders.

When I met Dana White in spring 2009, I knew very little about MMA or the UFC. In fact, I could barely watch boxing. Still, I was convinced to take the meeting because I'd been told the UFC was up-and-coming and I needed to meet this Dana White character behind it all.

I walked into the UFC headquarters, and there were huge images everywhere of bloody fights and roundhouse kicks and everything else that makes me uncomfortable. Good start. Dana arrived shortly thereafter in jeans and a vintage T-shirt and sat down at a conference table that I was sure cost twice as much as my car. He swung his feet up on the table.

"So, I hear you're the Twitter Queen," he started.

I admitted that apparently that was my name around town.

"Listen, fans don't give a f—k what I'm doing all day," he insisted. "It's boring sh-t."

I replied that they do care and it's not boring. "What did you just do before this meeting?" I asked.

"I reviewed T-shirt designs, and they sucked. I told my creative team to try again."

"What if you took a photo of the designs and asked UFC fans—the people who are buying the damn things—what they think of the designs? Wouldn't that be easier than guessing what they like?"

He was quiet. Now that I had Dana's undivided attention, I explained the benefits of personally embracing social media for the UFC.

I learned he is not one to pull punches—it's something I appreciate about him. He is, like Shaquille, incapable of faking anything. He is who he is across any communication medium, and that's a perfect recipe for social media success if your audience values what you bring to the table. I knew he was a perfect fit to humanize the UFC brand with its fans. And I told him so.

Fortunately Dana is a renegade. It didn't take any coaxing to get him going. My primary role was helping him understand how to make the best use of these huge communication channels in order to promote the UFC brand. I gave him two need-to-know pieces of information at the outset.

First, I told him that social media is not a marketing tool. You have to earn the right to sell something in the same way you earn the right to ask a friend a favor. If we just met and I asked you if I could borrow fifty bucks for dinner, what would you think? You'd think I was tacky, first of all. And you'd probably conclude I was pretty self-consumed, even if I asked with a Cheshire grin. That would set a distasteful tone for our relationship from the get-go. Not exactly the path to lasting loyalty.

The other need-to-know I gave Dana is that social media is not a popularity contest. Followers don't automatically equal influence. Succeeding is not a volume game because friends, fans, and followers don't directly translate to income on a profit-and-loss statement. Impressions don't convert, but influence does. And gaining influence cannot be contrived. It requires an unprecedented (and potentially uncomfortable) level of accessibility and exposure.

Traditional marketing and PR are ultimately less and less effective because they are merely creative forms of monologue that don't invite people into connections with other people. Only dialogue sticks because it is one thing to gain an audience, and another thing to keep an audience by reinforcing your relationships with real people every day. To be successful with social media, you must choose to compete on how much value you can offer and how much trust you can build with fans. If you get those right, loyalty becomes tangible.

Dana embraced the advice from day one. He engaged with fans' tweets, answering their questions directly, thanking them, and surprising many with his candor. He shared personal details of his day, including interactions with the fighters hours before their fights. He was shockingly honest. Fans ate it up. So did Dana. Connecting with fans became more than a strategic obligation. His connections with fans were the clearest gauge of his brand's strength. He even began keeping the national media in check by calling them out via Twitter if they reported stories incorrectly or didn't give credit to the proper source. Fans came to trust his information before any journalist covering the sport.

Dana became so convinced of the value of social media that he invested in Digital Royalty training for more than three hundred UFC fighters, which included financial incentives attached to their social media performance. The more popular their tweets were, the more they could earn.

One of the earlier strategies for going deeper with UFC fans was the result of serendipity. It was a case of fortune favoring the renegade.

SHAQ
@SHAQ

Don't believe what u read if I say something it'll be on TNT or tout dnt let idiots persuade with yellow jou...
tout.com/m/l3oneb

28 Feb

Dana White
@danawhite

@SHAQ that's why I love social media!!!! Squash all the BS from being misquoted, taken out context and flat out LIES. Talk direct to people.

↩ Reply   ⟲ Retweet   ★ Favorite

2:26 PM - 28 Feb 12 via Twitter for iPhone- Embed this Tweet

Dana was responding to a fan directly, via a direct message, or so he thought. He tweeted his direct office phone number to the fan, inviting him to call to continue a discussion they'd begun over Twitter about tickets to an event. Dana just wanted to provide personal assistance. Only he didn't send the tweet directly to the fan. He accidentally sent it to all 1.5 million Twitter followers who quickly retweeted his number to their followers and so on. Within minutes an estimated 9 million people had his direct office line.

I was in another city doing something other than thinking about the UFC brand when I received a frantic call from Dana. He went straight to the point: he'd

Dana White
@danawhite

:-D my pleasure. Call my office 2 morrow
702 221 4781

↰ Reply   ⇄ Retweet   ★ Favorite

floated his private office number into the Twitterverse and needed me to delete the tweet.

Can't be done, I told him. He paused.

"Well," he replied, "if I'm stupid enough to tweet my phone number to everyone, I'm going to take their calls."

For the next forty-five minutes, his phone rang nonstop. He took as many calls as possible. Some callers wanted to see if he'd actually answer. To their delight, he did. Others had questions to ask or comments to make. To their amazement, Dana listened and replied. It was an audacious move for the president of a billion-dollar enterprise who, in the mind of many executives in his position, had more important matters to attend to. It also turned out to be a legendary move. Headlines were made, and engagement levels spiked.

The next day my team and I reviewed the impact this had on the UFC's online ecosystem. Dana had struck a chord. I called him and shared the numbers and then told him my team felt there was something more to be done. I suggested he set up a dedicated fan phone on which he took calls regularly. He immediately approved it.

Suddenly thousands of fans who were mere voyeurs of the sport became engaged with the brand on a regular basis. Not getting through to Dana didn't seem to discourage anyone. Fans seem to equally enjoy the experience vicariously through the tweet reports of those who had, jumping in with questions about what he was like and what was said. The UFC was quickly becoming more than a pay-per-view event to plan a party around. The brand was a live person you could relate to and talk to, and he listened and cared enough to respond. Followers became raving fans in droves. Over the next few days, Dana added thousands of Twitter followers and Facebook likes. Most important, he gave the UFC brand a community that was cemented in authentic connections that both parties enjoyed.

Eventually we took the concept beyond Dana. With marketing partner Boost Mobile, we provided the fighters with fan phones as well. This made the concept monetizable and more scalable, allowing fans to connect with more of their UFC heroes more frequently.

The UFC community grew to be so strong that when Dana famously called out a detractor for his coarse remarks, fans didn't flinch:

In fact, they did the exact opposite. Dana added a great many new followers in the two days that followed. So much for the notion that exposure at the executive level is bad for business.

Dana White
@danawhite

@92Brougham I give a shit about the fans. I don't give a shit about u! Get off my twitter and never watch ufc again

← Reply   ↻ Retweet   ★ Favorite

3:09 PM - 10 Apr 10 via web - Embed this Tweet

In the rough world of MMA where only the toughest survive, Dana being Dana has been nothing short of brilliant branding. Which probably leads you to this question: How does all this Dana being Dana translate to the bottom line?

It's an important question and one I'll let Dana answer. You play the marketing executive.

About two years ago, Dana was having dinner with a marketing executive friend. It was the eve of a major UFC event, and Dana was explaining to him the enormous benefits of social media. *Fans are engaged like never before. Feedback is instant and constant.* He was not being shy about his adoration.

"That all sounds nice," said the marketing executive. "But what about the bottom line? Can you show me there's an actual return for all this?"

"I don't know how to quantify the return," replied Dana, "but let me show you something."

Dana then proceeded to tweet that in five minutes he would be at the gas station across the street from their restaurant. The first one hundred fans to show up would get free tickets to the event the following night. Dana showed the marketing executive the tweet he drafted.

He paid their bill, and then the two walked across the street to the gas station, and Dana hit Send. Less than one minute after their arrival, the first eager fan showed up and claimed his free ticket. A few minutes later, more showed up. Then more. And more. Within fifteen minutes, more than two hundred fans showed up. One by one they received a ticket from the UFC president's hand.

At some point in the midst of it all, Dana turned to his inquisitive friend and said, "How's that for an f—ing return?"

Ask yourself the same question.

That kind of loyalty adds up quickly.

Social media can change the way you innovate and scale your brand if you let it. That starts by realizing that setting up Twitter, YouTube, and Facebook accounts is not going to cut it as your social media strategy. You need to free yourself up to seeing social channels as communication opportunities, not advertising opportunities. Let the connections and conversations serve as your best advertisements—because they are.

I realize that not every brand can break onto the social media scene the way Dana White did. Not every brand audience will necessarily be receptive to the primary personality traits of the top brass. But every brand audience has relational values they hold dear. I mentioned the most common ones earlier in the chapter. But that list is not exclusive. Your audience may value entertainment as much as anything else. Find a person or people connected to your company who are incredibly entertaining, and give them liberty to connect with fans in the social space.

Maybe your audience is centralized as a cohesive group and values community involvement. If you're the CEO or president, take fans with you real time as your business invests in your community. Invite them to offer more ideas and even get involved.

Many brands break into the social space using Twitter accounts as channels for customer relationship management and customer support, managing pissed-off or happy customers in near real time. This may be your best first play. Tony Hsieh, CEO of Zappos.com, is a classic example. He humanized Zappos through social media by leading with accountability when mistakes were made with online orders. Zappos has effectively extended its brand promise of stellar customer service into connections between customers and employees who solve their problems in real time. These connections give customers a forum for providing feedback when, where, and how they want to share it. Next to a face-to-face interaction, it is the most tangible way to turn negative experiences around and amplify positive experiences, and both have an impact on the bottom line.

Zappos **Zappos.com**
CEO **@Zappos_Service**

@makoskim We have an wonderful Community Involvement team. Please use this link:about.zappos.com/our-unique-cul...

Zappos **Zappos.com**
CEO **@Zappos_Service**

@makoskim If you follow us, we can DM. I will be happy to give you more information.

Zappos **Zappos.com**
CEO **@Zappos_Service**

@nyMari Woo Hoo.... happy to hear that you like your new sandles!

⬅ Reply   ↻ Retweet   ★ Favorite

Because Zappos.com and Tony have spent twelve years focused on building strong relationships with their customers, they were able to survive something that could have potentially crippled them when 24 million customer accounts were compromised by hackers. The incident was revealed through a tweet sent out by Tony's @Zappos Twitter account as well as company blog:

Zappos **Zappos.com CEO-Tony**
CEO **@zappos**

I sent the following security incident email
to Zappos employees today: http://bit.ly/xRxQfd

← Reply   ⟲ Retweet   ★ Favorite

5:30 PM - 15 Jan 12 via web - Embed this Tweet

Exposing yourself through social media need not be accompanied by flares or fireworks. You don't have to release a sex tape or offer a scandalous dig on somebody famous. Remember that it is not about gaining attention but keeping attention. Often it's the simple invitations into everyday occurrences that give fans the truest encounter with the humanity behind your brand. Affinity can come at any turn, but it most often comes at routine turns. In the end, we are more similar than different.

While I was at the Phoenix Suns, I was constantly getting my hand slapped for trying to recruit everyone from the mascot to the president of the company. HR said, "Hold up, there has to be a company out there that has a policy in place." I'd heard about Zappos.com's commitment to social media, so I direct-messaged (DM) Tony Hsieh and asked him if he could share his social media policy. The only reason I was able to DM him is that at the time, Tony followed everyone back who followed him. Two weeks later, I received a DM from him that stated, "Be real, and just use your best judgment." I thought to myself, *Wow, man of few words*. Turns out those eight words are Zappos.com's company-wide communication policy. A month later, Tony visited Scottsdale for a speaking engagement, and that's the meeting that eventually led to our working together.

A couple of years ago, I developed fuzzy vision. In one week, I had attended six sporting events but couldn't read the scoreboard or clearly see the court or field—and I was wondering if there were others in my audience who shared my pain. Turned out a few thousand of them were in the same boat.

When I saw the surprising number of responses, I took the conversation deeper. Had anyone been through LASIK surgery, or did anyone have any experience with it? Was it for everyone? What were the downsides? Did it hurt?

The conversation evolved further and people began sharing their personal experiences—what they've heard about LASIK surgery and what life is like with and without contacts and glasses. Most responders were grouped into two categories: those who had LASIK and those who were considering it but were hesitant. People weren't sure of cost, recovery time, or the process in general. Neither was I. As the conversation continued, a Phoenix-based ophthalmologist, Jay Schwartz, joined the conversation.

Schwartz and I had been acquaintances since my days with the Phoenix Suns since he is the team's ophthalmologist. With an invitation to come in for a consultation (along with an endorsement from former NBA superstar Grant Hill), I quickly obliged. And I took my followers with me every step of the way.

After sharing photos and tweets in real time during the consultation appointment, Dr. Schwartz came in to discuss my options and ultimately let me know whether I was eligible for LASIK, which I was. I tweeted the good news, and then showed him the conversation that had been generated about LASIK. What happened next?

 # Dr. Jay Schwartz
@DrJaySchwartz

Yep, you're a go. RT @DigitalRoyalty: Hopefully @DrJaySchwartz says LASIK is a go. http://yfrog.comeiggqj

The story didn't end there. A couple weeks later, my (virtual) LASIK friends and I returned to Schwartz's office for surgery. Because I obviously couldn't tweet during the procedure and immediately afterward, my team and I made the decision to talk Schwartz into allowing us to live-stream the surgery for my LASIK community. After some gentle persuading, he graciously gave us the green light to go live on Ustream.TV. I let my community of 1.2 million know the time and date, and together we went under the laser. It was an unexpectedly bonding experience that many followers used as a catalyst for their own LASIK procedures.

In the end, showing some skin is more natural than you might think. It's no different from meeting someone at a cocktail party and spending a few minutes getting to know one another through conversation. The only difference is that you probably know a little something about your audience already. Perhaps you're acquaintances, but to this point you've never gotten closer. This is your best opportunity. You can't get to know someone better without revealing something more about yourself. Eventually both you and your audience will become more comfortable with sharing more, but you must lead. You set the tone that determines how connected you become.

After my surgery, my LASIK tweeps and I felt more deeply bonded, the way you do after you take a trip with someone. We had a unique bond based on a shared experience. The more of these your audience can have with your brand, the further you can go together and the more you can accomplish.

If you're still shifting in your seat, remember that showing some skin is not about transparency. It's about truthfulness. I don't recommend the full monty on social media, which will almost always do more harm than good. Spilling your guts isn't a good loyalty strategy; it will just freak people out.

You don't need to share everything. You can be selective about what you expose as long as what you decide to reveal holds real value for your audience. And if you're not sure what your audience values, ask them. Chances are good they value more than one thing that you or your business also values. There's your conversation starter. From there, one onion layer at a time. The more layers you peel back, the more values your audience will reveal. The more values you know, the clearer your business growth becomes.

But don't get too far ahead of yourself. Show some skin, but make sure that skin is yours.

RULE 3

Unmask Your Motives

Innovation Allergy: *Vulnerability*

I n 2007, Tiger Woods's favorability rating among American adults was 83 percent according to a Rasmussen Report. Between December 16 and 20, 2009, the same survey was conducted again, just weeks after his many transgressions became public: Woods's favorability rating had plummeted to 38 percent. No shocker there.

A bit more than two years later, on March 16, 2011, the same poll, undertaken again by Rasmussen, Woods's favorability rating had dropped even more, to 31 percent. You'd think the passage of time would do some good for the image of what had been the most popular athlete on the planet. Not the case.

Maybe a little more time was needed.

In early April 2012, just before the Masters and just after winning his first tournament since 2009, his favorability rating was still a paltry 34 percent—four points lower than when his indiscretions first became front-page news.[1]

So why hasn't Tiger been able to return to our good graces? Are we the general public really that unforgiving?

No. We just don't like insincerity.

"Tiger Woods's personal brand took a big hit in 2009 when his sex scandal revealed how little we really knew about golf's biggest star," summarized John Paolini, partner of the New York branding agency Sullivan.

So he wasn't that squeaky clean athlete we all thought. But we've been disappointed before, haven't we, Mr. Clinton? And yet the president, in 1998, the same year his indiscretions became public knowledge, received the highest approval rating of his entire presidency: 74 percent. When he left office, his 66 percent approval was, and still is, the highest rating for any exiting U.S. president in history.[2] One could argue that Monica Lewinsky actually strengthened Clinton's brand. I don't think that, but it's an interesting theory.

So what's happening here? We all know, as Paolini reminds us, that "scandalized celebrities certainly make comebacks—they repent, they reinvent themselves, and they come back better—with more valuable brands than ever."[3] In Gallup's 2011 favorability poll of recent and current political playmakers, Bill Clinton scored a higher rating (61 percent) than President Barack Obama (52 percent) and was second on the list to only First Lady Michelle Obama (66 percent).[4] So then why hasn't Tiger made his comeback?

The simple answer is that we still don't know what makes Tiger Woods tick. We don't know who he is other than that he likes women and can play a mean game of golf. When he skipped the pretournament interview for the 2012 Wells Fargo Championship in favor of a video Q&A session he released on his own, it was "a decision that reeks of paranoia," wrote sports journalist Robert Lusetich, "a clumsy attempt at controlling the message. It also gives the impression—rightly or wrongly—that Woods wants to dodge tough questions." Woods, he continued, has largely been "estranged from the media that covers him, and when he needed their restraint at the end of 2009, he instead got their revenge."[5]

The more complex answer is that he has given us no other reason to like him than for his performance—and his performance has yet to return to its pre-2009 form.

Many businesses unknowingly put themselves in a similar situation when they opt out of social media or simply dip a toe in without any intention of diving in. Customers know them only for their performance—their quality clothing or specialized products or stellar customer service. If the main measure of performance maintains its edge—if the service remains stellar, for instance—loyalty can hold steady. But it's more like a unicycle-on-a-tightrope steady than a tank-on-flat-ground steady.

Here's why.

While the base value of any brand still relies on performance today, how much value depends on more subjective attributes like charisma, courage, attractiveness, and candor. Said another way, being excellent still earns an audience these days, but to keep them and attract more requires giving them something more personal.

If your brand delivers green jackets, great customer service, or high-quality goods, it can establish a baseline value. But if that's your brand's only source of loyalty, it will be tougher and tougher to maintain in a world where quality is often equalized at the top and your primary competitors' brands are increasingly personified with qualities people can relate to, associate with, and learn from.

Without the ability to nurture loyalty through human connection, your brand's value relies solely on performance. When your market takes a dive or your products lose a step, your fans have no heartfelt reason to remain loyal because the basis of their loyalty is gone. Right now that's what is happening with Tiger. Had he taken to social media with honesty and candor when his world came crashing down, it wouldn't have healed things right away, but his favorability would not still be at 34 percent more than four years later.

What if instead of demanding privacy and dodging the media's questions, Woods called himself out to his followers? It wouldn't need to be sappy, which isn't his style anyway. He could just make himself the butt of a joke. It's very disarming when people who've screwed up make fun of themselves. When an extortionist threatened to take David Letterman's Tiger-like sins public, Letterman confessed on his show. "Would it be embarrassing if it were made public?" he quipped to his audience. "Perhaps it would—especially for the women."

What if instead of reading a prepared, emotionless statement at a press conference, Tiger went Shaquille style and recorded a video that went directly to his fans? I'm sure he would have loved a reason not to take the stand at a press conference.

What if instead of disappearing from the game and laying low for three months, he took his fans on the journey with him and gave them snapshots of what he was going through—the good, the bad, and the ugly? No need to disclose every gory detail. Imagine how a tweet like, "Sloppy day on the range today . . . emotions got the best of me," would have gone over with fans.

If you don't think we would have been rooting for his overkill comeback, you probably thought the movie *Rudy* was melodramatic. May your cold heart find a remote glacier to call home.

If he'd shown at least some emotion, wouldn't we have felt at least some of Tiger's pain—despite the fallout being his own fault? And wouldn't we have been more inclined to offer compassion? Wouldn't we have believed in him again sooner, perhaps even more than we did before, because, after all, he was suddenly a lot more like us because of his faults, not despite them?

Of course, we would have. Why? Because we are all human. We've all been the dog. And we've all wished for compassion and forgiveness a time or two.

It's pretty safe to say that I've kept many agents and publicists awake at night. I've worked with many over the past few years, and more times than not, healthy tension arises when a social media expert advises the celebrity to do everything his or her agent and publicist have asked the celebrity not to do: "Share your personal stories and interests." "Talk about your hobbies." "Post behind-the-scenes photos." It's a new age, and if the celebrity or CEO doesn't share this content, it's likely someone else will, often in a different light. The content will have the most credibility if it comes first from the source. You can either own your brand or live in fear.

Tiger's brand has not yet returned to favor because it wasn't human in the first place. It was mythological: the golf god with laser focus and an obsession with perfection. When it turned out there were other things he was focused on and obsessed with, the myth unraveled. We suddenly had a down-to-earth lens through which to see him. The problem was that he chose to continue carrying himself as though the myth remained intact.

Although Tiger has more than 2 million Twitter followers, his communication remains largely void of real emotion. That's another way of saying we still don't know what makes him tick. As a result, his brand value remains bound by his performance, or lack thereof, on the course.

He'll continue to get endorsement deals as long as there is hope that he'll return to golf dominance. Will the deals be as lucrative as they once were? Not as long as the only things he can endorse are brands with a high-society or high-performance message. Family-friendly brands and character-based brands won't be calling unless something changes.

"So what?" you might say. "What if Tiger doesn't want to care about social media? He's a professional golfer, after all, not the president of the Elks Lodge."

Fair enough. It's a common response I hear from executives and celebrities: "Why should I care about people getting to know me? I run a business, not a dating site."

True. If you're a professional golfer, or a business owner, or a company president and you're not good at it, you need to find another career. So do what you gotta do to win tournaments. Do what you gotta do to keep making great products and hiring great people. Sure, you're a _____ (insert job title), but if you're on your game, aren't you also an entrepreneur?

In order to make the most of your business, you have to constantly keep your eyes peeled for opportunities. If you're an athlete or celebrity, you know the great value in endorsement deals, so shouldn't you strive to be endorsement friendly? If you're a businessperson, you know the real money is in licensing deals and corporate partnerships, so shouldn't you strive to be a brand other brands want as their partner?

The most annual income Tiger ever made on the golf course was $11,515,939 in 2005. As of the end of 2011, his career prize money totaled just under $100 million. He's not eating a lot of Top Ramen, in other words. Yet in that same span in which he made $100 million on the course, he earned more than $900 million off the course through endorsements, course design, licensing fees related to his video game, corporate outings, and so on.[6]

Here's a pop quiz for you:

Pop Quiz

If Tiger was a business, what should he give his attention to?

    A. His golf game ($100 million)

    B. His brand value ($900 million)

    C. Both

This isn't a trick question. He obviously can't ignore his golf game because that's the skill that gives him a global platform in the first place. In the same way, you shouldn't ignore the skills that keep your business on its A game.

But can Tiger ignore $900 million in income in pursuit of a better and better golf game? I suppose he can if he wants to. But there's only so much prize money available. If he won every tournament he entered in a year, the most he could take home is between $250 million and $300 million.[7] It's a great goal to shoot for, but really, is he ever going to pull it off? Are you ever going to land the business of every available customer in your market? Not gonna happen, even for someone whom many think is the greatest golf player ever. In his best year, 2005, Tiger took home roughly 4.5 percent of the total prize money available (approximately $11 million of $250 million available).

Of course, if Tiger is an entrepreneur, he knows there is a much simpler way to make that kind of money and more. So the correct answer to this pop quiz is: C. Both.

And just in case you're thinking Tiger's brand value is self-perpetuating and he doesn't really need to work on it, consider this. Since the fallout of late 2009, the value of Tiger's brand has been on a downhill slope, falling from nearly $110 million in off-course income in 2009, to approximately $72 million in 2010, to $62 million in 2011.[8] With numbers that big, it's difficult to feel the pain of a 44 percent decrease in brand value in two years. But if your company's sales income was nearly cut in half in two years, you wouldn't be flying the company to the Bahamas for a celebration. You'd be figuring out a way to stop the bleeding. Pronto.

The solution for Tiger is the same as for any business that wants more lasting and more lucrative loyalty: expand your business strategy so that your growth is not based solely on performance. The best brands are built on loyalty to something much more visceral than products or services. Yes, they have quality products that provide them a national or global platform. But these brands' value is built on loyalty to their purpose.

Ultimately, people don't buy what you do; they buy why you do it.[9]

First Who; Then Why

If today's primary branding question is, "Who is your brand?" then the next question is, "Why?"

Let me explain.

In a brilliant TEDx talk, author Simon Sinek described the primary differentiator between brands that lead their respective industries and everyone else.[10] Most businesses, he explained, brand themselves by starting with the clearest thing first ("What we do"), move to "How we do it," and finally work toward the fuzziest thing ("Why we do it"), which is often the default answer, "to make money."

If I was a run-of-the-mill auto business and I was pitching my brand, it would go like this:

1. I would tell you *what* my business does: "We make desirable cars with great gas mileage."

2. I would then tell you *how* my business accomplishes this: "Our cars are made with the finest materials on the finest equipment in the world."

3. I would end by telling you *why* my business does what it does: "We want to earn your business. Would you like to buy a car?" That's code for, "My motive is your money in my pocket."

You might buy a car from me, and if you still like that car after a few years, you might buy one for your son or daughter. But I doubt you're a fanatic about my cars. You're about as loyal to my brand as you are to that restaurant where you had a good meal the other night. You might eat there a couple of more times and then you'll find something else that suits your taste just as much. There are plenty of good restaurants, after all.

Ultimately, you don't have any deep-seated attachment to my brand. It's only a car, and there are other desirable cars with great gas mileage made with the finest materials on the finest equipment. Why not try one of those?

In contrast, the most innovative brands with the strongest, most lucrative loyalty brand themselves in the exact opposite way. Here's how they pitch their brands: Why, how, and then what. It goes like this:

1. They tell you *why* they do what they do: "We believe there is always a better way, and we always aim to find it. We believe in thinking differently."

2. They then tell you *how* they do what they do: "Because we think differently, we marry cutting-edge technology with human intuition and beautiful design to create products that look and function like no other."

3. Finally, they tell you *what* they do: "We sell computers. Would you like to own one?"

This completely different approach works because people become loyal to the brand's intent, not merely a product. It gives companies like Apple a visceral connection to their fans, which allows them to sell more than computers. Can I interest you in an iPad, iPod, or iPhone too? If you're an Apple loyalist, you probably have them all.

Every great brand, concludes Sinek, sets out to find other people who believe what they do. Loyalty is strongest there. Knowing this, great brands get crystal clear on why they do what they do. They are just as resolute about sharing this information with their audience. The branding process starts with why.

And this is where social media comes in:

- These are the ideal tools for brands to convey why they do what they do in an efficient, humanized manner.
- They allow brands to quickly identify and stay connected with people who believe what they believe.

Why Share Your Why?

There are two basic presumptions behind every excuse I've heard for doing social media only partially. You think who you are is either none of people's business or irrelevant to your success.

The first presumption is a favorite of high-profile celebrities and sports superstars who use protecting their privacy as an excuse for detachment from fans. Kobe Bryant is a classic example. He launched a Twitter account in 2011 and had thirty-five thousand followers in the first three hours. He freaked out when he saw the numbers and realized he was suddenly accountable to say something. He shut down the account. According to Bryant, it was "released prematurely." Nice.

That's the choice every brand faces today.

Everyone has a personal brand, from my mom (@BlackHillsDiva) to *Time* magazine journalist Joel Stein who interviewed me in 2010 for an article on self-branding. To get started, I asked him to describe himself: "Lazy, self-involved and sexually frustrated" were his answers. I told him "lazy" was really "needing stimulation," which was really just another way of saying "dynamic," which was just another word for "rock star." "Self-involved," I told him, was really just "open." Starting to get it, he then suggested that "sexually frustrated" is really just "sexy."

I replied, "I think the first two for sure. Remember, Joel, your ultimate personal brand audit is your funeral. If you see a need to make some changes to your brand, do it now."[11]

The second presumption, that social media is irrelevant for success, is a favorite of many smart but nearsighted executives I meet. I was once sitting in a meeting with a CEO of a major brand, and he stopped me midsentence and said, "Wait a minute. You want ME to tweet?" I replied yes, and he rolled his eyes as if I'd asked him to play hopscotch. To him and others like him, I simply say, "Well, if your best opportunity to strengthen customer loyalty in the quickest manner on the smallest budget is irrelevant for success, I guess you're right. No argument there. I'll shut up now."

The problem with both presumptions is that for either to be true, you ultimately have to conclude that people in your audience don't care about your motives. In fact, the opposite is true. Everyone—you and me and everybody in between—cares about intent more than anything else, especially the intent behind the brands with which we associate.

Most brands mask their motives because they haven't thought it out. But when a brand comes along that is willing to drop the mask, we're often sold on their what and how before a product is even pitched. TOMS Shoes is a perfect example.

While on a trip to a remote part of Argentina, Blake Mycoskie, TOMS's founder, discovered that many villagers, children mostly, couldn't afford a pair of shoes. As a result, they faced health problems and could not attend school. He decided to do something about it. In 2006, he created a simple pair of shoes, based on the traditional alpargata design that Argentine farmers have worn for hundreds of years. It was one style in a few popular colors. His intent was that for every pair he sold in the United States, he'd give a pair to a child in need.

TOMS launched its business, and people flocked to get their hands on a pair, not because they were the best-looking or most exquisite shoes. They were, in fact, very simple looking and inexpensive. Rather, they believed in the brand's intent to help children in need. Buying a pair was about sharing and collaborating instead of spending and consuming. There's an enormous difference when that switch is flipped in the minds of your audience.

Amy:Digital Royalty
@AmyJoMartin

Just ordered 14 pairs of @TomsShoes. 7 for the Digital Royalty team & 7 for kiddos in need. We love TOMS. Rewarding shopping.

Veronica Belmont
@Veronica

@Digital Royalty so really, you donated 14 pairs to kids in need, because Toms already donates a set when you buy!

↩ Reply ⟲ Retweet ★ Favorite

5:10 PM - 2 May 11 via Twitter for Mac - Embed this Tweet

In 2011, while giving the keynote address at the annual South by Southwest Conference, Blake unveiled the next TOMS product, sunglasses. In keeping with the brand's one-for-one intent, he explained that for every pair of sunglasses sold, the company would give a needy child sight-saving medical care, prescription glasses, or surgery. In less than forty-eight hours after ninety different locations began selling the sunglasses, several styles had already sold out in all stores and online. As Virgin magnate Richard Branson has written, "Doing good is good for business."[12]

That kind of response has little to do with the product—the what of the brand. It also has little to do with the process—the how of the brand. That kind

61

of response was about TOMS's intent—the why of its business. The truth is that TOMS could now sell roller skates if there was a place in the world that was desperate for them. Next thing we know, it'd be time for an international "all skate."

When intent is hidden in a person or a brand, we suspect there's a reason, especially in a world that makes sharing intent so simple. But more important, loyalty is not anchored very deep.

In my interactions with many celebrities and decision makers for big brands, I've found that the number one reason people have such a hard time unmasking their motives through social media is that they fear their motives aren't truly pure. That's not to say being motivated to make money is morally wrong; it's just that you know you're not going to sell a lot of anything if you tell customers you're all about the money.

The truth, however, is that nearly everyone I talk to has a deeper reason for doing what they do. Sure, they want their brand to be wildly successful and make money, like any of us would want. Last I checked, that's the goal of every for-profit business on the planet. The real issue is that they haven't given enough thought to their why, if they ever have at all. They have done precisely what Simon Sinek says most average businesses do: they've downplayed or skipped the fuzzy why question and snuggled up with the what and how of their brand. That's the way it has been for a long time: "We sell _____. They are made of the finest _____ with the finest _____. Wanna buy one?"

That's not how it is anymore. Those who want to win over and keep an audience today have to dig deep and then adjust to the new way of doing things. There are countless competitors in the marketplace with a similar, if not the exact same, type of service or product offering. Your brand's intent and personality are the differentiating factors.

That said, I can understand the challenge. Humanizing digital royalty isn't always easy.

Why Is Where What You Do and How You Do It
Gain Meaning for Your Audience and You

As I've already said, when I was a kid, my family moved quite often. New states, new schools, and new sets of friends every couple years led to my addiction to change.

Several months after I left my Suns job, I was running a fast-growing agency that specializes in developing social media strategies and customized training curriculums for many notable brands. I was traveling the world attending fancy client events and speaking on social media measurement and innovation. Almost every day, major media outlets wanted to talk to me, *Forbes* named me one of the five most powerful women on Twitter, and I was jet-setting across the globe, often flying in private planes. From the outside looking in, it was perfect. But a chasm was forming between who I was and what I did for a living.

Then during a jog one morning, I was listening to the Simon Sinek TEDx talk I mentioned earlier. Somewhere in the middle of it, he posed an interesting question that stopped me in my tracks: "If you don't know why you do what you do, how do you expect people to follow you?"

Suddenly it was as if the universe was flashing bright lights at me. I could almost hear, "U-turn! U-turn!" Something was off, and Simon's question hit me over the head with the answer.

Why *was* I doing what I was doing?

The answer didn't roll off my tongue, and I knew it should. I knew it wasn't all about the money. So what was my work about? If I didn't know, how could I expect people to follow me or my advice?

I'd spent two years helping celebrities and high-profile brands become more influential by teaching them that the process of developing their brands begins with sharing their intent through social media. I'd encouraged them to be real with people. *Unmask your motives*, I'd told them. *Don't be worried about the value proposition at the outset. We'll figure that out next. Right now, you want people to follow you for a deeper reason than what you do (dunk a basketball, make movies, sell clothes) or how you do it. You want people to follow you because of who you are. So show them who you are.*

In my own way, I was instructing them to start with their whys. And yet when I heard Sinek's words, I realized I hadn't been completely heeding my own advice. I'd boarded 210 flights in one year and averaged four hours of sleep each night—and now I found myself mentally and physically exhausted, sometimes unable to remember my home address. Until that point, I thought I adored what I did for a living. I'd conveyed as much on Twitter and Facebook numerous times. My business was my passion and my baby. My lifestyle was a constant party. Work hard, play hard. Yet all of a sudden, I was disenchanted with this thing I had given absolutely everything to. It had a good financial return but not good fulfillment. I had strayed from my why—if I had ever known it in the first place. I was creating a Frankenstein-like brand that was becoming more and more detached from who I was. The what and how of Digital Royalty had masked the why.

I began sharing my feelings with close friends and family. That's the point when they started saying, with loving tension in their voice, "You need more balance, and you need to slow down."

Ah, yes, of course. Those words were like fingernails on a chalkboard. I was allergic to slowing down, and balance was counterintuitive to innovation and progress.

Then my hand was forced, and I had a choice to make. After not feeling well for several weeks, which I chalked up to exhaustion, I paid the doctor a visit. My white blood cell count was abnormally low along with other levels that were out of whack. I had a golf ball–sized lump in my breast. It was a scary moment. It was also an opportunity. Time to take up the challenge I was laying down for everyone else.

Without giving everyone too much information, I let my Twitter followers know what I was going through. I battled with the words. I'd let my followers in on a lot of my professional life, the advice and tips, and some of the fun parts of my personal life, but none of it was this personal. I let go anyway.

Things are busy. For everyone. Sometimes our pace tends to flirt with near recklessness. I was in New York for business meetings, and I told my life managing director (my magical assistant) that I wasn't accepting any more meetings for the day. My calendar was closed after a healthy load of fifteen meetings and a business dinner already scheduled. Next thing I know, I see another meeting request pop up in my e-mail in-box. Seriously? Deep breaths.

The meeting request was titled "Ready, Set, Pause . . ."

Little did I know that Alana and Jessica from my team had a behind-the-scheduling scenes scheme going on to help me out. They brilliantly scheduled an eight-minute reprieve to reset, refocus, and relax.

The value in taking this eight-minute meeting was unbelievable. The return was unmatched. I put my headphones on and listened to two mood-matching yet altering tunes from my "Innovate Your Life" Spotify playlist that Alana created. I now find it's irresponsible for me to miss a "Ready, Set, Pause" meeting with myself. We've made it reoccur daily in my calendar, and it's a priority. Sometimes we have to shift the meeting, but there's always time to reschedule for that day. Eight spare minutes can be found in the day. If not, two four-minute sessions work well too.

I started encouraging my social media audience to take a #ReadySetPause break with me, and the feedback was incredible. People were really grasping this concept and implementing the simple yet rewarding exercise into their daily routine. *Forbes* even covered it. Apparently we are all desperately in need of a daily reset.

My intent was to connect in the way I was instructing my clients to connect—to let people see that I was more than the "Tweetheart" *Vanity Fair* deemed me or the social media powerhouse *Forbes* said I was.

I was shocked by the overwhelming response, including messages from many of my clients:

Dwayne Johnson
@TheRock

Blessings.. @AmyJoMartin "Good news today. Cancer free. It's been a wild ride over the past 5 months. Attack & #Livestrong"

↩ Reply   ⇄ Retweet   ★ Favorite

12:26 AM - 29 Sep 11 via web - Embed this Tweet

The support I felt from my online community was powerful. I had leaned on them while running a marathon, tweeting back and forth after each mile. But this was a more intimate challenge. Raw. No fluff. Thankfully, after surgery and quite a few months hopping from doctor to doctor and test to test, the lump was removed, and it was benign. But I took more from that experience than the news that I was healthy. I also took away a significant lesson.

I realized that unmasking my why was reframing what Digital Royalty did to not only my followers and the company's clients; it was also reframing Digital Royalty to me. The job that had usurped my health became the very thing that would give it back to me in spades. The brand that offered social media strategy was becoming the brand that championed innovation, renegade style, through social media.

This exercise freed me up to be my same self on and off the job. No longer did I need to keep up appearances. It wasn't that I was being fake. It was that I was holding something back that was a key to my company's success and significance: I was letting my perception of what the market wanted influence Digital Royalty's identity instead of letting that identity be tied directly back to me, its founder and CEO. A little more light was shed on my purpose. Few other moments have been more freeing in my life.

While lunching with Simon Sinek shortly after hearing his talk, he asked me to recall my first childhood memory, good or bad. I recounted skiing with my family for the first time. We skipped the bunny slope altogether, and my dad took me straight to the top of a double black diamond, a scary straight-down slope. He instructed me to make a pizza shape with my skis and then put my skis between his. Like that, we navigated our way to the bottom.

On hearing this, Simon asked, "Has it ever occurred to you that you've never been a bunny slope type of person? Very possibly your why is to help people do very difficult things in their lives." I now have one tattoo. It's on my wrist—a sketch of two black diamonds. A reminder of why I do what I do. You may not need a tattoo, but you will need a consistent reminder and lifetime commitment to your why.

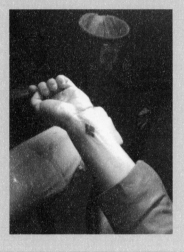

Imagine building a business off your being yourself. And imagine that ongoing action being a significant piece of your business's bottom line. Would it change how you felt each day you came to work or the way you thought about your business?

Integrity and *innovation* aren't two words that come up together in conversation often. But those two words, taken together, are the bookends of all social media success: a brand that is authentically human, constantly ignited by the innovation that comes from human interactions given the freedom to collide, explore, and collaborate.

Loyalty between people—whether between two friends or between a business and its customers—rarely happens until the intent of each party is clear and a common foundation is then created that they can share. Once that foundation is established, loyalty is firm and scalable as long as you are willing to remain in that uncomfortable place where it all began, regularly sharing some skin and unmasking your motives.

I'll give an example in the next chapter.

RULE 4

Get Comfortable
Being Uncomfortable

Innovation Allergy: *Change*

was attending another Ultimate Fighting Championship (UFC) fight,
sitting across the ring from Dana White on media row. That's when
I received a text from Dana that said, "Come over here now." *Great*, I
thought, *what did I do wrong?* I walked around the ring, fingers crossed. When
I got there, Dana immediately pointed to the big guy standing next to him and
introduced me to The Rock.

I had an epiphany as we shook hands, which is another way of saying I'm
about to confess something. I had seen the celebrity list for the fight that night
and noticed "The Rock" on the list. But I couldn't recall who that was. Okay,
I thought it was referring to Nicolas Cage who I knew had played the lead in the
movie *The Rock*. Honest mistake.

Before I finished shaking hands with this "other" Rock, Dana turned to him
and launched into a pitch about how he had to embrace social media and how
it was the best thing ever and about how I was the Twitter Queen who could

show him exactly what to do. Dana is convincing, but I could tell The Rock was nodding to be nice.

"I have to tell you," The Rock confessed, "I'm a very private man, and I'm really not comfortable blending my personal life with my professional life."

It wasn't the first time I'd heard that sort of response, and it certainly wouldn't be the last. I told him as much and then conceded that using social media wasn't something you could force. You have to want to do it, I said.

"But remember," I continued, "this isn't the paparazzi. You have full control over what you put out there."

I then explained that social media ultimately made his brand, and rough-around-the-edges charisma, more scalable in that he could reach more fans on a more frequent basis. It also allowed him to do more good on a grander scale, and in the end, it could actually be enjoyable.

He was probably feeling a little peer pressure when Dana jumped in as soon as I finished talking and insisted I set up The Rock on Twitter right then and there between bouts. The Rock consented and then his associate, Hiram, who was standing nearby, leaned in and suggested he check with the rest of his team and publicist first. Good call in this situation, actually. The Rock brand is made up from a team of people, so what he does has an impact on that entire team, whom he respects and trusts greatly.

We finished talking shortly after. The Rock took my business card and said he'd be in touch. I wasn't sure we'd talk again and headed back to my home base on media row.

One of Digital Royalty's responsibilities during live UFC events was to share that night's story virtually with fans watching from all around the world. A big storyline in each night's live event—and I attended more than fifty of them—was always who was in the crowd. My job was to show the fans. I quickly learned there's an art in approaching a celebrity and requesting his or her photo. It was a one-two punch, if you will. First, communicate their WIFM ("what's in it for me") within the first five seconds. Second, make sure they knew they had the chance to approve the photo. (A few celebrities, who shall remain nameless, had me take several photos from different angles and requested I use my fancy iPhone Photoshop app for a little extra polish before we deployed their mug out into social cyberspace. Fair enough.)

The WIFM was the UFC's social media influence on their side—millions strong. This was valuable to them, and most celebrities, from Ashton Kutcher and Demi Moore (back in the day) to Steven Segal, Janet Jackson, and Tom Brady (tough gig I had that night), realized it. My social leveraging skills have never been turned down (knock on canvas). The UFC's WIFM was that the celebrities would also share the photo, and sometimes video if I played my cards right, with their audience. This introduced the UFC to a new audience and lent a natural endorsement by that audiences' idol—the celebrity. It positioned the UFC as "cool" straight from the celebrity.

Two weeks after the fight. I received an e-mail from a Dwayne Johnson. I thought, *Dwayne who?* I opened the e-mail and saw it was from The Rock. (Of course!) He wanted to talk more about social media. Fortunately, staying in a comfort zone wasn't his style. He recognized an opportunity when he saw one, and after a couple of more chats that included his manager, agent, publicist, and assistant, he jumped in with both feet.

I've since become friends with The Rock (I now call him "DJ" because neither "Dwayne" nor "Mister The Rock" ever felt right). He's become a rare branding force in the global community with more than 9 million friends and followers who are as diverse as anyone else I've worked with. He just had to overcome that initial hesitation.

Today the amount of attention DJ gives to social media, along with his hands-on approach, is unmatched in the world of celebrity. He works at it daily, and it's always his fingers to the keyboard or iPhone. Nobody speaks on his behalf. Ever. DJ is successful with these communication channels because he's dialed in and has fully and personally committed to delivering value to his audience.

You may be where DJ was at first, and that is understandable. It's not traditional protocol to bring your personal life to work, and it's not comfortable. Plus you have a polished, professional image to uphold. But what

Dana White and I once spoke at Harvard, and he proceeded to say to the students, "No business suit ever made me any f—ing smarter." The tendency to conform everything from policies to dress codes just because "that's the way we've always done it" couldn't be more of an antiquated approach. Dana White, his billion-dollar company built from scratch, and his vintage T-shirt–wearing ways have proven that we can color outside the lines without crossing the line. I personally donated most of my business attire and suits after leaving the world of professional sports. I prefer my Spiderman and The Rock #TeamBringIt T-shirts.

does that really mean? Has anyone ever asked? Are we all expected to stuff our personalities into a business suit every time we cross the office door threshold?

I can't speak for everyone, but I enjoy a little personality around the office. And the businesses I enjoy working with the most are usually the lively, eccentric ones. Are your favorite brands "professional"? That's not the first adjective that comes to my mind. Sure, a level of professionalism is required in any business interaction. But that doesn't mean you can't exude a little individuality.

I've spoken to many entrepreneurs, celebrities, and executives who get that social media has value. They even agree that the best brands have a human quality to them. But often it's that first leap toward a new protocol, or culture shift, that gets them hung up. They just can't see themselves sharing their lives with thousands of people, let alone millions.

Yes, putting yourself out there feels uncomfortable for most people. But this isn't exactly public speaking we're talking about. Forget imagining your audience in their underwear—*you* can be in your underwear and your audience will never know. Besides, any renegade knows that no risk worth taking is without some discomfort.

In fact, if every business decision is easy, you're probably playing it far too safe. You're playing not to lose rather than playing to win. Staying on your game requires constant adjustment. And change is never comfortable, at least not at first.

So get comfortable with being uncomfortable. Own it. With more than a billion people using these communication channels, you can't afford not to have an active role in the conversation.

A Trade Worth Making

During my time leading Digital Royalty, I've found that the most successful people and brands resolve to make the same trade-off. They trade comfort for momentum. It's not that they embrace discomfort. Nobody likes stress, anxiety, or embarrassment. It's that they understand that avoiding stagnation in any endeavor takes an ability to get used to—to grow comfortable with—growing pains. Today's renegades are not unlike adrenaline junkies who feed off the knowledge that the highest highs can be had on the backside of our biggest fears, anxieties, and chaos.

Where social media is different from say, BASE jumping (that is, jumping from fixed objects and using a parachute to break the fall), is that social media becomes far easier and wholly invigorating once you've reaped the rewards. Diving off a skyscraper wearing only a backpack? Never easy.

Fast-forward a year from our first meeting, and DJ enthused that embracing social media was one of the best things he ever did personally and professionally. Fast-forward another six months, and DJ had become a leader in the social space with a higher retweet rate—the percentage of his tweets that are re-sent by his followers to their followers—than most other celebrities: 11 percent.[1] To give you an idea of how huge this rate actually is, a 3 percent retweet rate is typically considered a success. Practically speaking, this means that approximately 300,000 followers have forwarded his message on to their followers. And it doesn't stop there. How many people from that base of 300,000 forward the message on to their own follower base? And then how many from the next and the next? It's an enormous ripple effect that according to my sports and entertainment friends at Twitter headquarters is unrivaled among his contemporaries.

All this should come as no surprise if you know anything about DJ. He has that rare combination of immense generosity and intense strength. He's also a renegade who has no problem taking risks, which was to his advantage from the beginning. A recent example of this was a hurdle that arose during the filming of G.I. Joe.

Before I describe that incident, I should bring you up to speed on how in less than two years DJ went from not having a Twitter account to having a loyal following of more than 2.7 million followers and more than 6.5 million Facebook friends. How he did it reveals a straightforward template for growing any brand's following—even if you're starting from scratch and your name isn't The Rock.

DJ's social media strategy started, as it should for anyone else, by defining his audience and his value to that audience. It wasn't as broad as breaking people into World Wrestling Entertainment (WWE) fans, moviegoer fans, and military fans, the primary places where he'd gained mainstream exposure. It was a matter of breaking down the psychographics of those different groups and assigning them to smaller categories based on their primary affinity to DJ's value and what resonated most with them. What was their WIFM?

Because DJ had been in the movie industry for years and also had a large WWE fan base when we started, we had some basic information to work with. For instance, we knew that more men than women were professional wrestling fans, and we knew their core demographics. We also knew that DJ had female fans from his action films and younger fans from his family-friendly films. While we certainly refined our understanding of each group as DJ's social media presence grew, this was a good place to start.

However, the most beneficial way to get our fingers on the pulse of who was in his diverse fan base was also the most logical thing: we listened to them directly and in large volume. We listened to the conversations fans were having among themselves about DJ, his projects, and his personality. We also listened to what they were saying directly to him. (You can now eavesdrop at any time and it's respected; it's called *listening*, and nobody has to know you are doing it.) When you listen, things become obvious. Sentiment, next steps, and ideas are exposed in a way a formal brand study could never deliver. These conversations are alive, they're real, and they're happening in real time. The trends identified could have never been garnered in a quicker, more accurate, or inexpensive (they were free) fashion.

Eventually DJ's audience groups looked like this, which is an actual slide from the digital brand audit we presented to him one day at his kitchen table:

Once these were defined, DJ's primary focus was on delivering value to each audience when, where, and how they wanted to receive it.

But how? How do you offer custom value to one audience without turning off another? You can't. So you don't. The value delivered isn't about what you are doing; it's about who you are. Dwayne Johnson, the person not the personality, is the one constant for his brand. People want to know who that person behind The Rock personality is. DJ is the one common denominator of value, what differentiates him from everyone else. It's also what keeps his value balanced, whether he's filming a "shoot 'em up" scene for an action movie one morning, sharing an inspirational quote that afternoon, and then telling a dirty joke that evening. It's about who he is in the midst of what he is doing. Delivering DJ's unique personality was and still is the content. If you have an affinity to someone because of who he or she is, are you far more likely to like what that person is doing even if you didn't like it before?

That said, the specific value details are initially educated assumptions that are clarified and adjusted over time. For instance, where DJ was concerned, we knew we could safely assume his male fans would find his fitness advice and behind-the-scenes action photos valuable, and his female fans would like seeing his softer side and perhaps pictures of him without a shirt on, and so on.

While each social content value offering (tweet, post, or update) always fell into one or more of the six value buckets, the preference was always to offer something that more than one audience category found valuable. These value buckets or type of offering are not the same for everyone:

VALUE BALANCE

EDUCATION ENTERTAINMENT INSPIRATION EXCLUSIVE INFORMATION RECIPROCATION

If you were now to look at DJ's tweets over a twenty-four-hour period, you would clearly see that he was hitting each of these value buckets.

Initially, removing demographic barriers, increasing his audience, and engaging them in ways they valued was a matter of educated trial and error. Some content didn't cause as big of a splash with any audience category. Others caused a tidal wave across multiple audience categories. DJ learned quickly and always adjusted his offerings toward what worked. Obviously this served as confirmation of what his fans wanted. DJ also remained creative and open to trying new ideas.

In a matter of a few weeks, we were able to create content templates for each audience group and determine which value buckets resonated with them the most. These templates encapsulated the specific types of content that that group most valued. Although these were always prone to change given ongoing audience feedback and the activity reports we provided DJ, the adjustments were easy to make and the templates easy to update. For instance, we learned that DJ's "action fans" valued exclusive behind-the-scenes details from movies he was filming or photos of particular stunts he was asked to perform—but only if DJ's point of view, humor, or personality was injected into the message.

Keep in mind that because social media is a dialogue, you can ask your audience what they value at any point. You'll get answers, and people will be grateful you cared enough to ask. But even if you get it wrong now and then—and you will, just as we all do—the beauty of social media is that followers are quite forgiving if you've built that relationship up first and you've earned it, especially when you can make up for a flat offering with one that's well received—and especially when your audience knows you're listening to them with a desire to deliver what they value most (I discuss listening in greater detail in Chapter Six). Suffice it to say for now that great listeners are never short on friends or followers. Listen loudly.

DJ's audience grew quite fond of him online.

With the advent of these progressive communication channels, celebrities who were once segregated from the masses by red carpets and paparazzi walls are now interacting in the same world as everybody else. Celebrities who take time to respond to fans are building their brand day after day. From the fan perspective, it's as if we're receiving our personal meet-and-greet or autograph but instead of "best wishes" on the back of an event program, we're being handed a customized message worthy of a boastful retweet, refrigerator post, or even a frame on the wall.

Fans benefit from the increased ease and connection with their idols, and those idols benefit from allocating less time and effort to garner the same amount of positive sentiment, press, and increased fan affinity as they would by connecting with them in the physical world.

Thom Gibbons
@CMMobileThom

Wicked day, @lfc thrash Bolton with a superb team display and now the legend @therock replies to my qestions on #rocktalk.

↩ Reply   ⟲ Retweet   ★ Favorite

27 Aug

Tom Ball
@TomBall1985

@CMMobileThom you got a tweet from @TheRock ?! That is awecome, you should definitely think about a new job as a reporter!

28 Aug

Thom Gibbons
@CMMobileThom

@tomball1985 I was well chuffed, thinking about puttingit on my achievements section on LinkedIn!!!

Well chuffed? Anyway, he grew just as fond of them.

Dwayne Johnson
@TheRock

I do now! RT: @julezmcgum: "@Laughbook: ❐ Taken
❐ Single ✓Mentally dating a celebrity who has no
idea you even exist." @TheRock"

Once the foundation of a two-way, dynamic relationship with his audience was established, the real fun began. By constantly delivering value when, where, and how his fans wanted it, DJ was able to consistently increase his reach (larger following) and deepen his existing followers' loyalty (greater engagement)—two goals of every business on the planet. Pushing our audience up one notch on that loyalty ladder can be priceless and make the difference between hitting a quarterly revenue goal or not. With social media, reaching them is limited only by your ability to innovate and execute (you've no doubt heard those words before). With social media, they are no longer loaded terms that make your stomach churn. They come alive with significant meaning. And the rewards are much easier to achieve and much quicker to measure.

While we are always trying out new and creative ways to increase DJ's reach and deepen his fans' loyalty to this day, a few campaigns have stood out because they demonstrated just how much influence he has. With your own personal touch, they might spark some ideas for your brand. And before the "I don't have enough time to play these social media games" excuse creeps into your head, remember that DJ is a busy guy. So are the pope and President Obama, and *they've* personally embraced these channels. Are you brave enough to make it a priority too? Here are two ideas we used for DJ that can help your brand get started.

#RockTalk

On August 27, 2011, DJ began offering fans a regular opportunity to communicate with him in real time. The format was simple: any fan anywhere in the world could tweet a message to DJ, and for thirty minutes, he would personally answer every question he could. The first ever half-hour #RockTalk garnered 13,800 mentions of @TheRock on Twitter—an average of 460 mentions per minute. During that time, DJ added approximately 9,400 new followers. Even more astounding was that the #RockTalk hashtag became the number one worldwide trending topic (meaning that the term is one of the most populated and popular terms on Twitter) within minutes of the inaugural session and remained on the top ten list for forty-five minutes. To put that into context, there were more than 300 million users on Twitter at the time, and the worldwide trending topic list garners hundreds of millions of impressions each day but publishes only the top ten most popular topics being tweeted about at any given time. Advertisers pay $120,000 and more to have their product, brand, or campaign on the trending topic list for twenty-four hours at a time. DJ didn't pay a dime. Just over a year after embracing a social media strategy, he had already earned enough influence with his audience that they placed his brand on the list organically within minutes of launching his first #RockTalk Q&A.

Less than three months later, DJ's influence with fans had grown even more. Just prior to appearing on the November 14, 2011, live TV broadcast of the WWE Raw event, he tweeted that he was going to make three words trend worldwide instantaneously. He then looked into the camera and spoke them. Within seconds "Boots To Asses" appeared on the top ten list.

DJ turned the tables with this stunt. Most marketers are trying to use social media to generate more people to turn the channel or turn on the TV, a common tactic for several years now. DJ instead drove TV viewers to his social media channels. He directed the viewership audience online, where it had a larger potential reach. He stretched a national audience into an international conversation that dominated other worldwide conversations happening simultaneously. That's a renegade. Why? Because it takes guts. It's a risky move to say something is going to happen worldwide within seconds of your proclamation. We didn't know for sure that it was going to trend worldwide. But we had confidence in

Dwayne Johnson
@TheRock

Seconds from electrifying RAW. Time to feed the beast and make 3 words trend worldwide.. #BootsToAsses

↩ Reply　　⭍ Retweet　　★ Favorite

Trends: Worldwide • Change
#LeaveYourLegacy ✉ Promoted
#iwannabe
#WishTheyWouldBringBack
#CenasLadyParts
#HottestPeopleOnTwitter
Boots To Asses
REASONS TO LIKE ME
Midlife Crisis
WELCOME TO MY LIFE
NEGASDAMADRUGADA
Crimen y Castigo

13 hours ago via Twitter for iPhone
Retweeted by IamGreerald and
100+ others

DJ's historical influence levels and then took the leap (some would call it a "calculated risk").

This would have never happened if DJ didn't willingly participate in the creative process. He was involved in the script writing and planning of this stunt. We understood what was going on and what was at risk; he also understood the likelihood of pulling this off because he had been personally listening to his fans day in and day out. He had been having a dialogue with fans, not performing a monologue.

Hide and Tweet
During the premiere weekend of his movie *Fast Five*, my team helped DJ coordinate ten hide-and-tweet stunts throughout the country on the same day of the movie release. The rules of the social media game were simple: fans had to follow him on Twitter to receive clues about where golden tickets were hidden. (We hid them under rocks.) The first fan to find each of the hidden tickets in each city received passes to the film as well as a personal phone call from DJ.

Thousands of fans in each city remained glued to DJ's tweets for a chance to claim the prizes. Without fail, the hidden tickets in every city were discovered within minutes of publishing the final clues.

Engagement was high and increased throughout the campaign. But even the first stunt started with a bang. It generated thousands of tweets the day of the actual movie release including more than one hundred retweets of @TheRock tweets. Fan sentiment was overtly positive, with some fans wanting

Ryan
@guyzwitgunz

@TheRock Hide & tweet, that would have been so fun and it's great u are doing this for the fans. Good luck with whatever u got planned 2nite

James Bignall
@BiggersUV

@TheRock great concept of the hide and tweet. All the best tonight, have a good one...

...who dis woman?
@kia_who

so @TheRock just played "hide & tweet" in ATL?? i'm so. damn. jealous.

joanne jayme
@jiwa13

@MichiezWorld @meners767_01 OMG did you guys c @TheRock's Hide & Tweet ticket giveaway? sooo jealous! when he's in the bay we gotta do it!!

giveaways in their home towns and others expressing appreciation for doing giveaways where they lived.

Impression Versus Influence

For decades, marketing success has hinged on making the biggest, most creative, most audacious impression. If you can make a big enough imprint on a person's mind, the thinking goes, you can move him to action to consume your product or service, vote for your candidate, or support your cause. The primary target of this marketing strategy is the mind of the consumer. The primary activity is shooting messages at the targets. The best shot wins. Right?

Not anymore.

"The most successful companies in business today have something in common," writes my fellow *Harvard Business Review* contributor Mark Bonchek. "This trait . . . makes them fundamentally different. Where traditional companies push out messages and products, these companies pull customers in. Instead of treating customers as passive targets, they treat them as active participants."[2]

In his insightful post, Bonchek goes on to provide three examples of brands that clearly have what he calls successful "orbit strategies," which create gravity that pulls customers to their brand: Apple, Google, and one of Digital Royalty's favorites, Nike. The fundamental difference between a brand like Nike and traditional thinking brands, says Bonchek, is the difference between pushing and pulling. Nike does not push its offerings at consumers like an archer shooting at a target. They create an attraction-based brand strategy that draws consumers in like planets around the sun.

"At the core of each orbit strategy," explains Bonchek, "is a platform or service, what might be called a Customer Gravity Generator." As examples, he cites Apple's iTunes and iCloud, Google's Gmail and Google+, and Nike's NIKEID and its latest offering, Nike FuelBand.

I was one of a select group asked to attend the live unveiling of Nike FuelBand, which counts running, walking, and all other activities of your athletic life. Nike FuelBand is calculated the same way for everyone, so you can compare and compete with anyone. For the first time, Nike announced this product over Twitter in addition to its standard PR methods. As the date of the unveiling came closer, Nike executives teased news outlets and Twitter followers with hints about what the product would be. They even leaked a video that gave people a taste of the big announcement. Gravity creation at it best.

Heidi Burgett
@heidiburgett

My FuelBand mission: Play tennis inside Grand Central Station yfrog.com/nzauycbj

↩ Reply   🔁 Retweet   ★ Favorite

Then on the day of the big reveal, I sat in a dark room buzzing with excitement. Athletes, celebrities, journalists, and major company executives all awaited a glimpse of this secret product we'd been hearing about.

Jimmy Fallon interrupted the buzz with a brief introduction and then handed the floor to Nike's president and CEO, Mark Parker. Nike vice president Trevor Edwards then revealed the new FuelBand.

Edwards explained the goal behind the product: to innovate and inspire athletes. Then, without further ado, he unveiled the FuelBand, an unrivaled fitness product you wear on your wrist that uses oxygen kinetics to track each step you take and every calorie you burn, which it turns into your "fuel score," a measurement of your day's fitness against your predetermined goals. I like to call it a scoreboard for life. And for added value, the FuelBand is integrated with social media outlets like Facebook, Twitter, Foursquare, and Path, so we can all share our progress and motivate each other as well as challenge Facebook friends on total fuel points scored per day. It is a product made with every athlete in mind. And according to Nike, if you have a body, you're an athlete.

Credible and elite athletes such as Lance Armstrong, Kevin Durant, and Carmelita Jeter took the stage after the big unveiling to humanize the product and then, in a brilliant move, each of us in the room was given a FuelBand to test around Manhattan for the day.

While participating in the event was an honor, impressing us wasn't Nike's point. With the FuelBand launch, Nike was creating what Mark Bonchek would call a "customer gravity generator." This wasn't merely a company shooting its new product at us, a pool of influencers with a large reach, the target market. When Nike invited those of us in that room to the unveiling, it was a brand inviting us into its gravitational field with a value offering that would improve our lives. They weren't trying to persuade us with a sales proposition. They were offering us value in hopes of earning our trust. That's where influence begins—it's a different result from an imprint.

Nike has a method to its product launch madness. These aren't just fancy release parties to schmooze media. They're well-thought-out master plans, mapped out to the last arrow and sign. If you were invited as a social media influencer, my gig, you were directed to a certain path because Nike knew this group of individuals would get news and content out to their audience first. They were instant influencers, versus the bloggers or print journalists who would need to write their story and have it approved prior to sharing their experience relative to the new product. Smart. In addition, strong wi-fi, laptop charging stations, and other technology details were conducive to spreading their sexy news. Want to post a link to live video during the unveiling before Nike gets a chance to post theirs? No problem. Fire away. Nike fosters an environment for sharing its content like no other. Especially if you're an instant influencer.

Laurie Thornton
@lauriethornton

Congrats. #FuelBand has really fueled the brand.

19 Jan

Alana Golob
@AlanaGolob

@Otis: Want to have a calorie burning face-off on 2/22, Otis? @Nike @HeidiBurgett @AmyJoMartin

19 Jan

Otis Kimzey
@otis

Who says social doesn't sell. Just pre-ordered two @Nike Fuel bracelets based on #makeitcount, @heidiburgett, and @AmyJoMartin's coverage

19 Jan

Allen Davidov
@AllenDavidov

@AmyJoMartin @nike love #nikeplus. Use it daily and will admit you've peaked my interest!

↩ Reply   ⇄ Retweet   ★ Favorite

18 Jan

Sure, Nike could have produced an expensive commercial, paid another $4 million to run it during the Super Bowl, and banked on a small percentage of viewers being impressed enough to hop online or run to the store the next day and buy one. It's a tough sell, and it doesn't really invite anyone into any sort of relationship. It's a hit-or-miss proposition that will have to be followed with another hit or miss.

Brands that aim themselves and their products at their market make little more than temporary impressions that have to be replicated over time for loyalty to exist. And keep in mind that you're not the only one taking target practice on your consumers. After a while, we all get tired of being fired at.

Here's another pop quiz:

Pop Quiz

Would you rather your brand make an impression or earn influence?

    A. Impression

    B. Influence

    C. Both

This one is a little trickier than the first pop quiz. Impressions are not a bad thing—they're just no longer the best thing and should never be the main thing. Businesses have for decades relied on getting inside the customer's head, and their artillery is marketing campaigns. A certain number of sales is the typical sign that the arrow hit the mark. The trouble is that it usually takes more than a few quivers full to hit a small number of target customers.

Renegades flip the traditional strategy around. They focus on becoming the target their customers are aiming for. Instead of aiming outwardly, they focus being someone the customer values inwardly. Instead of firing, they aim to be inviting.

It just so happens that human beings are the best sort of inviting, both influential and impressive. Humans make mistakes; therefore, being human is not always comfortable. It's just more credible.

Aim for influence first. Impressions will come as a result because influence converts. Impressions rarely do by themselves.

RULE 5

Ask Forgiveness Rather Than Permission

Innovation Allergy: *Rejection*

t was a Thursday afternoon a few years back when I received a call from a Washington, D.C., number I didn't know. On the other end was a notable senator's chief of staff. News of this senator's affair had leaked, and now the chief of staff wanted me to "do some social media magic" and make it all go away.

"Can't we just create a viral campaign?" he asked.

No, I told him. The audience, not the messenger, decides what goes viral. We can't just create something on YouTube, for instance, and tell millions to watch it.

The conversation then progressed to what could be done. I told him that it all begins with intent. Why did they want to embrace social media in the first place?

Two reasons, he said: to measure how bad the public sentiment really was and to mitigate the damage to his boss's public image.

The problem? The senator didn't have a presence on the popular social channels to begin with. I knew we couldn't just create an account and have him hop on and begin tweeting about how he loved America or how passionate he was about a certain bill—or how regretful he was for what he'd done to his wife.

> In the interest of full disclosure, after the call I immediately reverted back to my days in social studies class and did some online refresher research on the government branches and the difference between senators and representatives. After a Google session, I realized this senator was kind of a big deal. Was I in over my head? Possibly, but that's when I'm often the most comfortable. Still, I couldn't believe I was one of the only people he could reach out to. Weren't there experienced political professionals who could have advised this chief of staff? Turns out there weren't.

"You could get after social media right away," I explained, "but for it to have any chance of helping the senator, he'd have to be completely real and forthright about his actions. No scripted messages. No beating around the bush."

The chief of staff said he needed to have a couple of conversations. We agreed to reconvene on a conference call that Saturday morning. In the meantime, I had a few conversations of my own with family members and close colleagues. Should I get involved or not? I knew the primary challenge was authenticity. Historically, people in political positions don't exactly score high on the trust index. Deceit and double-mindedness are unfortunately things that no longer surprise us from Capitol Hill. Not judging here—just calling a spade a spade.

So in keeping with spades, the dilemma I faced was whether I was going to marry Digital Royalty to a cheating senator. I hadn't yet made up my mind when our Saturday morning call rolled around. Intuitively it didn't feel right, and that was how I was leaning. But if the senator was real and agreed to approach it the right way, I could see this as a potentially positive situation on many fronts, not the least of which was a very interesting experience that could prove to help others down the road.

As it turned out, I didn't have to make a decision (which ultimately hinged on the senator's willingness to come clean, not cover his tracks). The chief of staff and other staff members decided it was best to fight the battle the traditional way, where they were familiar with what to do and what to expect in return.

A few days later, the senator stood before a podium at a planned presser, suit fitted and every hair in place, and said precisely nothing of significance. After he was done, he took no questions and stepped away from the podium. There now. All done, right? Apparently it wasn't. The senator was eventually forced to resign.

Could social media have improved his standing and ultimately helped him avoid that fate? Yes, if he'd been willing to be a person instead of a politician. This conclusion is not difficult to come to. As we've already discussed, coming clean is ugly and unpredictable, but it's also real. And we like real. We also like comeback stories. What we don't like is insincerity. Right, Mr. Woods? You can't just jump on social media for damage control when you've never embraced it in the first place.

We all have the tendency toward the creation of a veneered version of our brands that we think is more acceptable, more compelling, more marketable to our audience. Traditional marketing has been about painting a compelling picture for decades—a polished veneer, so to speak—whether or not it was accurate. The irony is that the strategy now makes your brand less relatable and less reliable. Ultimately it makes you less human.

Here's why.

Veneered identities didn't have such backlash in the past because we the consuming public expected it and we played along. We gave our attention and money to the cleverest commercial, the sexiest billboard, or the funniest radio spot.

Now, the growing sentiment is that there's a better option. We *can* get to know a brand if the brand is willing to let us. If it's not, then it must be unreliable or trying to hide something. Heard that before. Doesn't it make more sense to embrace the better branding option than to risk appearing unconscious, uncaring, or untrustworthy?

The biggest hurdle for my potential clients, from popular sports teams to major corporate brands to A-list celebrities, has always been that this renegade form of innovation is difficult to tie down and put in a pen. Social media is raw and unpredictable. You never know what might come next. And what works—people being people—isn't perfectly safe. Progress revolves around experimentation, which means the rules, if there are any, are being written in the process. It also means you often learn through mistakes. But mistakes are okay if you are engaged with an audience and they've come to know who you are. The faults of a friend are far more forgivable and far more easily forgotten. You can count on that.

This is the paradigm that I've had to operate with from that first day I decided I would help the Suns players with their social media accounts despite warnings not to. Had I gone into "ask for permission first" mode, I wouldn't have learned how well social media can work for all of us. I also would not have ever left my cozy corporate cubicle. I'd have my dreams thumb-tacked all over my carpet walls, and I'd stare at them longingly each day. Okay, I'd like to think it wouldn't have ever gotten that bad, but I've been to the cubicle city section of many office buildings and I know it's not a stretch. So do you.

Fortunately I learned as a kid that asking for permission first wasn't the most efficient way to get things done. The answer was often "no," especially if I wanted to try something new. I learned, in other words, that innovation is not for permission seekers. It's for those who are bold enough to stick their necks out for a progressive, even zany idea and humble enough to say, "I'm sorry," or "I failed this time around," and mean it when they are wrong.

I can't say for sure, but I believe Digital Royalty is responsible for the social media policies being written for the entire NBA and Major League Baseball. I remember numerous times when I was with the Suns that we ran into internal dilemmas with social media, and the executives' natural inclination was to ask, in essence, "What does the rule book say?" I would have to remind them again and again that the rules hadn't yet been written and there were no precedents. Social media was too new and too few people believed in its viability anyway. Many were even crossing their fingers that what they viewed as a fad would eventually fizzle out. Meanwhile, we were making up the rules as the need to do so arose.

This wasn't what anyone in the front office of any large organization wanted to hear. But they came to learn that anyone who believed in social media and had an entrepreneurial bent couldn't wait for permission. I give kudos to the Suns organization because they ultimately went a little renegade and set the social media tone for the entire NBA.

When I was hired to work with the Chicago White Sox, Ozzie Guillén was the team's manager. Ozzie is a bit of a wild card. He says what he thinks and wears his emotions on his sleeve, for better or worse. He's not for everyone, but love him or hate him, you can always depend on his fearlessness to express his opinions. I already knew his reputation when I was hired, but my job wasn't helping him—yet. He didn't even have a Twitter account.

My job was to help Scott Reifert, the senior vice president of communications, build the White Sox team brand using social media. Scott, an early adopter, began blogging in 2005. The fact that he already got it made my job that much easier. Our discussions surrounded strategies for humanizing the White Sox brand, which for starters meant innovating ways for Scott to connect to White Sox fans. We were still discussing the best ways to get players connected.

Then one game into spring training, Ozzie's sons got in touch with me and asked for help setting up an account for their dad.

I thought it was a great idea. He fits the prescription for social media success—an individual who doesn't pull punches. With a little training, I felt he could really be an asset to the organization's brand on Twitter. I would learn, though, that Ozzie can be trained only so much. (I think it's safe to say others have learned this as well. But I digress.)

I helped Ozzie's sons acquire his official name on Twitter, taking it over from someone who was pretending to be Ozzie. I figured we would work on a strategy with Scott, train Ozzie, and give this a whirl. Wrong. Ozzie began tweeting almost immediately. Scott was not thrilled. Kenny Williams, the general manager, was not either. In their defense, we hadn't discussed Wild Card Ozzie tweeting and I understood their concern. Ozzie didn't ask permission or forgiveness, for that matter. He and his questionable grammar now had direct access to fans 24/7. ESPN was calling me to get the scoop on how all this went down, and I was once again in the hot social media seat flying solo. But ultimately we had to test the waters to see what would float and what would sink. In the end, our leader, Scott, wanted what I wanted, which was to connect White Sox fans to the humans behind the franchise's brand. Ozzie was certainly one of its primary faces. As we brought the players up to speed on Twitter, the well-rounded personality of the White Sox came into view, and fans joined in by the thousands.

Bring Your Results

Innovation is constantly evolving and the results rarely fit into perfect compartments. The materials that renegades use are often foreign, especially in the beginning. And that's not a bad thing. A home with hundred-year-old heart pine flooring is more appealing and valuable than one with laminate flooring. Like a weathered piece of wood, tried and true from the elements, the value of social media is in the bumps, nicks, and bruises that give your brand its unique humanity.

Innovation is messy, imperfect, and risky. But that's what makes it so effective. As much as we think we crave homogenization, we are consistently more compelled by distinction and diversity. The phrase, "Never a dull moment," isn't said in the company of clones. And last time I checked, brands aren't clamoring to claim the slogan: "Never an interesting moment."

It's a risky thing to embrace social media, but the truth is that nothing worth doing is without risk. This is something FOX Sports understands well.

When FOX Sports called Digital Royalty, it was immediately clear they planned to go big out of the gate. I love clients like that. They flew me and a few Digital Royalty team members to their studio in Los Angeles to attend their NFL and college football seminars and provide two sessions of tactical and strategic training for all the talent and producers. This was their all-in approach to getting their talent onboard with social media and educated within the space before the start of the 2011 football season. Going into the seminar, my team had prepared brand audits for the talent who already had an online presence, like Troy Aikman and Michael Strahan, who both had a strong social presence, and others, like Jimmy Johnson, who had none. I wanted to know where they stood on the whole so I could meet them right where they were. At that point, I'd done enough social media how-tos that I knew the why and what almost always had to precede the how. It was no different in this case.

I opened the first session for the talent and producers of NFL on FOX, which included Curt Menefee, Michael Strahan, Jimmy Johnson, Troy Aikman, Terry Bradshaw, and Howie Long, among others on both radio and TV. I spent thirty minutes catching them up on the social media state of the union, explaining why they should embrace it, breaking down their misconceptions, and then sharing a few athlete and celebrity case studies.

It was obvious who was ready to move forward and who wasn't quite ready to commit full scale to the space. Jimmy Johnson, for example, was in the all-in category. After the session was over, he came up to me and said, "I want to do this Twitter thing." He confessed that until that day, he had known virtually nothing about social media or Twitter specifically, but he was very interested in jumping in. My team sat down with him right then and there and installed Twitter on his BlackBerry, optimized his account, helped him pick his avatar, got his account verified, and then sat around him as he sent his first tweet—a photo of a giant marlin he'd recently caught.

The beauty of the tweet is that it was believable. Anyone who is a fan of Jimmy's knows fishing is his passion. After he sent out his first tweet, my team helped him find other Twitter accounts and personalities to follow, and his first question was, "Can I follow fishing accounts and other fishermen?" He was in it to gain just as much from Twitter as he was willing to give to it. We loved that. From his first tweet, Jimmy kept it real and authentic. He didn't try to sell anything or drum up support. All he wanted to do was connect with fans about the two things he loved: football and fishing.

Jimmy Johnson
@JimmyJohnson

@JenniferPransky@curtmenfee fishing next couple of days with son Chad.83 degrees.. here's what we're going to catch! pic.twitter.com/XgOyLThC

↩ Reply   ⇄ Retweet   ★ Favorite

Before we concluded our training that day, he already had a couple of thousand followers. And he was bantering with other talent on Twitter and responding to fans. He was a natural from the beginning. He continues to share his opinions on football and photos of fish he catches to fans who ask.

FOX Sports's strategy was to provide the proper training for the talent and then free them up to tell the individual stories behind the FOX Sports logo. This humanized the brand from the first day we began working together.

Because social media has an impact on all aspects of business, FOX Sports has also provided training for all departments across the company. It is now a major component of its corporate strategy.

On August 18, 2011, FOX Sports made a major announcement with the Ultimate Fighting Championship that brought the sport of mixed martial arts to the biggest sports network in the United States (yes; that's FOX Sports) over the next seven years. The announcement played out on social media and was syndicated across multiple channels. Here is how the strategy went down and the results went up:

This teaser to a big announcement is retweeted and/or replied to more than six hundred times:

Dana White
@danawhite

Good Morning! I have funny feeling today is gonna be a GREAT DAY!!!!!

← Reply   ⇄ Retweet   ★ Favorite

10:30 AM - 18 Aug 11 via Twitter for iPhone - Embed this Tweet

At 10:00 A.M. Pacific Standard Time (PST), the UFC director of communications sends a press release to thousands of members of the media. He shares the historic moment on Twitter via yfrog photo:

Prescott Miller
@presottmiller

Pic of @Sholler_UFC sending the biggest press announcement in @UFC history! One of the best days in my 5 year UFC career. yfrog.com/kfremvpjj

← Reply   ⇄ Retweet   ★ Favorite

2 hours 25 minutes ago

One minute later, the press conference goes live on Ustream, the FOX Sports Facebook page, and UFC.com. Immediately members of the media, like @DarrenRovell, begin live-tweeting the press conference:

darren rovell
@darrenrovell

Dana White says the "Ultimate Fighter" will be live on FX as part of new UFC-Fox deal

◄ Reply   ⟲ Retweet   ★ Favorite

3 hours ago via web
Retweeted by GlobalEd718 and 19 others

At 10:26 A.M. PST, "TUF" (short for The Ultimate Fighter) starts trending on Twitter in the United States:

Trends: United States • Change
#BeyondScaredStraight ▱ Promoted
#WorstThingInTheWorld
#WishTheyWouldBringBack
#imdigginthat
Paul Wall
Blade Runner
Ridley Scott
Abercrombie & Fitch
TUF
Poetic Justice

One minute later, "Ultimate Fighter" is trending on Twitter worldwide.

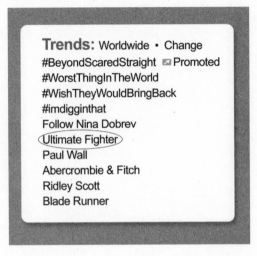

At 10:55 A.M. PST, 13,455 viewers have tuned in to FOX Sports Ustream channel to watch live.

At 10:56 A.M. PST, the new Twitter account @UFCONFOX Sports sends its first tweet with a photo from Studio 2A.

UFCONFOXSports
@UFCONFOXSports

You all ready for this!! Watch live on foxsports.com!
#UF #UFCONFOX yfrog.com/h8rubjkj

↩ Reply   ⟲ Retweet   ★ Favorite

5:55 PM - 27 Mar 09 via Twitter - Embed this Tweet

One hour later, @UFCONFOX has 1,270 new followers. Two hours later, that number has more than doubled.

At 12:23 P.M. PST, the @UFC sees a major spike in conversation with more @ mentions in two hours than the previous twenty-four-hour period.

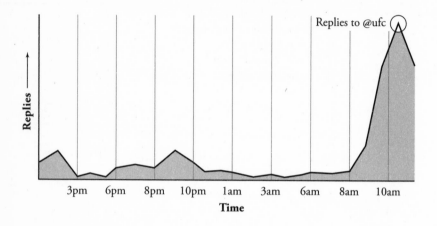

Knowing that social media has changed the way news breaks around the world, the UFC and FOX Sports leveraged real-time conversations when fans were most engaged to increase their social footprint, extend the reach of the news, and amplify their message around the world. The result was a deeply integrated, syndicated, and cross-promotional social PR win.

FOX Sports didn't ask for permission to change the way TV is done. They just did it and brought their results with them when anybody questioned if they were off their rocker. And those results are worth more than sentiment.

Social media can no longer be referred to as "added value." This is not like back in the day when ad agencies threw banner ads and e-mail blasts into their deals. The unique value that FOX Sports now offers to advertisers and partner brands is that its fans have a dedicated affinity to sports. With its social media strategy, FOX Sports has created a niche demographic within platforms that traditionally have very limited segmentation abilities without buying ads. These aren't hollow followers that don't convert.

FOX Sports's integration of social media and TV is valuable. This isn't the same thing as a TV promotion; FOX Sports is offering media buyers incremental value with its social integration, which offers higher targeted rating points at a lower cost per impression. Advertisers have very few options where they can get this same type of custom programming and viewership integration while directly tapping into the natural affinity of the viewer.

FOX Sports's trailblazing of the television experience demonstrates what can happen when a large corporate entity is willing to forgo the traditional permission that can sometimes take years. Television is actually the perfect medium to blaze trails with social media, but the going is still slow because very little has changed with the medium in sixty years. Historically the television box speaks outward in a one-way fashion, entertaining its viewers. Now the viewer has a direct pass to speak right back. As advertising brands and media outlets, if we're not listening and acknowledging, it appears we don't care.

Let the forward-thinking brands blaze ahead. Sure there will be some failures, but they will be learning the lessons for success and reaping the rewards just as their competitors are finally getting with the program.

It is no longer enough to slap Twitter handles and Facebook URLs on the TV screen and call it socially savvy television. Social media users can now dictate the outcome of live TV shows, create its content, and, most notably, boost the ratings.

Lessons for Renegades

Throughout the succinct two-year history of social television, successes and failures have taught practitioners three valuable lessons. In fact, these lessons apply to practitioners in any major medium (radio, film, television, journalism).

Keep It Organic

As you know by now, the golden rule of social media is to deliver value when, where, and how your audience wants to receive it. These words were first shared at a sports conference in 2010 by Bryan Johnston, chief marketing officer at the Ultimate Fighting Championship and former senior vice president at

Burton Snowboards. The beauty of social TV is that the audience is providing value right back. Naturally viewers are talking about their favorite (or least favorite) TV shows and sporting events. So let them talk back when, where, and how they want to. It not only provides a temperature on opinions and sentiment; it also extends content into a perpetual conversation kept alive even after the show is over.

For example, *The X Factor* realized that its highly enthusiastic following on Twitter had strong opinions about the show's contestants. The show's executives got in touch with Digital Royalty, and we helped them see that their viewers didn't necessarily care if the TV show itself was listening to their opinion; they were naturally sharing their thoughts, feelings, likes, and dislikes with their peers in the interest of a more personal viewing experience. That didn't mean it was okay to not engage them. We saw it as a huge opportunity to be immediately pursued.

Sydney Hill
@sydsbeauty24

I am tooooo emotionally involved in the X Factor! Now I 'm not I'm not beathing til Astro goes through to next week! Lol

← Reply   ⟲ Retweet   ★ Favorite

5:33 PM - 17 Nov 11 via Twittererrific - Embed this Tweet

We monitored their followers' social media behavior and listened to their viewers. Then we helped *The X Factor* become the first show to ever harness social media's inherent power and let viewers vote via Twitter direct message. This provided a convenient and direct means for loyal viewers to voice their opinions in a meaningful and yet official way. It also ushered them to a deeper level of engagement. Of course they'd want to see whether the one they voted for did—or didn't—survive.

Offer Low-Barrier Engagement

It's not a new concept for television shows to host contests highlighting viewer submissions to engage and create loyalty with viewers. However, with the evolution of social TV, the entry process has become more accessible. Instead of submitting something on a form, e-mail, phone call, or regular mail, viewers can almost instantaneously contribute to their favorite show using social media.

Jimmy Fallon is one of the pioneers of this concept. In the prehistoric age of social TV (a little more than two years ago), Fallon trailblazed by inviting fans to be part of the show by providing Twitter hashtag prompts to viewers and airing the most creative and hilarious responses on the air.

 jimmy fallon
@jimmyfallon

Let's play the hashtag game! Tweet out a funny or crazy superpower you wish you had and tag with #mysuperpower. Could be on our show!

↰ Reply   ↻ Retweet   ★ Favorite

3:15 PM - 2 May 12 via web

Why was this so innovative? It kept the viewers in their own space. Fallon's calls to action require little effort. A simple, witty one-liner in a tweet you were already going to send could be your chance at late-night stardom.

What was the benefit for the TV show? Viewers were now entertained at an incremental level. They were participating with the show and invested in the next evening's show to see if their tweet was highlighted within the broadcast. Simply said, they were elevated one notch up on the loyalty ladder. Many of the hashtags even became trending topics, which garnered accelerated awareness for the innovative hashtag game and, even more important, the show itself.

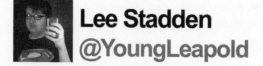

Lee Stadden
@YoungLeapold

I would make athletes call timeout when I need to go to the bathroom. #mysuperpower

← Reply   ⟲ Retweet   ★ Favorite

about 20 hours ago via Twitter

Raquel Calderon
@RccERRN

I would be able to close the elevator door as soon as I got in so I wouldn't have to pretend I tried to push the open button. #mysuperpower

← Reply   ⟲ Retweet   ★ Favorite

about 20 hours ago via Twitter

The show's new return on investment could be determined by hashtag counts, trending topics, increases in followers, and engagement levels. With more conversation around the show, more eyes are on the show's other tweets, which may include money-making advertisement-laden links, promotions, or other show initiatives. Heightened awareness means a greater reach and, in the end, a more profitable show.

Measure and Share Real-Time Results with Viewers

TV networks and shows can put their finger on the pulse of viewer engagement before, during, and after a show airs.

Historically, it was enough to say, "Most-watched show on Wednesday night." But that has little meaning for viewers. For them it just means they watch a popular show. In the end, it's vague and static.

Companies like Mass Relevance, Simply Measured, and Trendrr have developed tool sets that networks, shows, and advertisers can use to measure the impact their TV presence has on their audience. This type of instant feedback based on data has never been attainable prior until now.

With social media engagement, networks can also give viewers this intriguing information at any time during the show. This is an offering fans find meaning in, even if only for entertainment value. It's also a reminder for each viewer that he or she is part of a much larger community—maybe even a party. And it's just intriguing for viewers to see the rate of communication spike up and down based on different points in the show. They ask themselves, *Are others talking about what I'm talking about?* Or, *Am I out on a limb with this thought?* Now the network and the viewer can know what matters most and least to everyone involved.

It's traditionally believed that word-of-mouth is the most influential form of marketing. Accordingly, TV viewers and consumers have an interest and trust in each other's opinions. Consensus matters because it saves time and provides clarity. In the same way we look for book or music recommendations from friends, we can now turn to social media to hear about the next big thing or track what the majority considers the highest quality or best value or greatest experience. With this in mind, renegade media outlets are becoming valuable editors of the social media space, using their expertise to tell their viewers what they should be consuming according to general consensus. This strategy also proves valuable to advertisers who can make more informed decisions about when, where, and how they want to advertise on TV.

What is most amazing about all this? The jury is still out on social media in most corporate minds. Most are dipping a foot in. Few are diving in head first.

And the reason is as simple as your perception of risk and failure.

When I was a child, I ran away. Daily. The genesis of these frequent escapades was my addiction to curiosity. I'd explore the outskirts of my trailer park in Wyoming, Kansas, Arizona, or wherever else my family happened to live at the time.

Like clockwork, I would eventually get hungry or disenchanted and head back home around dusk. My parents knew the drill and never feared I wouldn't return—even when I was adamant that "this time I might not be coming back." I always provided the warning in the event I found something so spectacular that I just couldn't go back to our conformed society. I always knew there was something undiscovered out there and wanted to be the one to discover it and share.

Renegades experiment and fail early so when everyone else jumps on the bandwagon, their best practices are being polished while others' are just starting to fail. I attribute a great deal of my personal and professional success to this philosophy. Sometimes it's not about being the best or smartest; it's about being the first to try and the first to learn from failure.

 Amy: Digital Royalty
@AmyJoMartin

Take risks & fail early so when everyone else hops on the bandwagon their failing process begins when you're winning.

◀ Reply   ⟲ Retweet   ★ Favorite

The main thing about asking forgiveness rather than permission is to go about everything with complete authenticity. There's something endearing and acceptable about someone who puts it all on the line for something she believes in. Whether or not you agree with her, you have to respect the intent and the passion behind it.

That's the choice every brand faces with social media. Sure, you can wait and see. Will you go bankrupt in the next thirty days? Nope. Congratulations, you're safe.

Will you go bankrupt in the next three years? I'm far less sure about that one. At the very least, you'll be far less relevant than you are now. I'd go so far as to say that if you're vacillating on social media today, you're vacillating on your tomorrow—whether or not you see it now.

Ultimately the question at hand is whether you are willing to put up with a few mistakes in order to become a much stronger brand. Social media will never allow you to keep your ducks in a row every day of the year. But the great irony of fearing social media for the sake of avoiding failure is that social media actually makes failure far less fatal.

Make a major media-worthy mistake today without an active and proven level of engagement with loyal fans, and you're looking at a long road to recovery—if you can recover at all. Right, Mr. Senator?

Make a major media-worthy mistake today, with an active and proven level of engagement with loyal fans, and forgiveness will come much more quickly. You might even find people are more endeared to you after admitting a mistake and making amends. While people will continue to be surprised by a certain level of failure, no one is ever surprised by failure itself. But what is more surprising than anything else is when a person or a brand owns a mistake immediately and authentically. You can trust a person only so much whom you've never seen fail. And you can't trust a person you've seen fail and hide it. But you can implicitly trust a person you've seen fail and then own it immediately and progressively.

Today the crowd can make or break innovation, so the choice is yours. Innovate and engage the crowd—or attempt to innovate and ignore the crowd. I suppose you could also not innovate at all. Some risks are smarter than others.

RULE 6

Consensus Is the True Authority

Innovation Allergy: *Delegation*

When Marty McFly rode his hoverboard in the 1989 classic, *Back to the Future II*, I thought I was in love. Not with Michael J. Fox, but with the concept of a skateboard without wheels as my mode of transportation. I imagined flying to school and allowing my dog to hop on this magical creation. That didn't happen, but what did was this thing called the Internet, which made this other thing called e-mail affordable to the masses. But before the masses embraced it, there were a few years where the vast majority was in either wait-and-see or not-quite-for-me mode.

Do you remember when e-mail just wasn't your thing? Now it's hard to imagine we ever lived without it.

The point is that we tend to discount what we don't know—until, that is, we either venture out and try it or we eventually discover we are in the ignorant minority.

Access Leads to Affinity

My hand is raised right now. Many people think I'm a sports expert. Not so much. My expertise is in branding, research, and analytics. It just so happens that a good deal of my experience has been in the sports world. That said, people still expect me to know everything about every sport, which I don't.

To my dad's disappointment, I knew virtually nothing about NASCAR yet found myself with a hot pass to the Daytona 500 in 2011. (A hot pass is the king of all VIP passes in the world of racing. If there were backseats in those cars, they'd let you sit there if you had a hot pass.) My avid NASCAR fan of a father was slightly jealous of the laminated magic I wore around my neck.

I was one of those people who didn't understand, or better yet "get," NASCAR. Whether it was the complicated old points system (which recently changed. Who knew?) or just my lack of exposure, I was in the camp of those who secretly, okay shamefully, made fun of the so-called "monotonous day of left turns and mullets." But I eventually discovered how misled I was.

Due to a personal endorsement deal with GM and Chevy, I attended the 2011 Daytona 500 as a complete NASCAR rookie—so much of a rookie that I wore black high heel boots to this gig. It was my first-ever experience at a live NASCAR race, and I can't ever remember watching one on TV either. I knew nothing about the sport other than the fact that NASCAR had a very loyal fan base and its success revolved around the teams' marketing sponsors.

The Daytona was a great learning experience on many levels. I obviously got to know what makes NASCAR so exciting. I also learned why fans are so loyal. And I swear on my iPhone, I didn't see one mullet. But the most significant lesson is Rule 6, the topic of this chapter.

There I stood, a former NASCAR phobic by all accounts, suddenly filled with excitement, adrenaline, and loud engines—all the stuff that makes life fun. Was I actually liking NASCAR? Yes. What could bring on such a quick change?

I was given a more intimate experience with the brand by way of its primary consensus. I mingled with the loyalists, in other words. And when you meet passion face-to-face, it's impossible to ignore. There were several reasons I couldn't ignore people's passion for NASCAR.

For starters, drivers are unusually accessible. They do fan Q&As and autograph sessions *the day of the race*. The Daytona 500 happens to be the biggest day of the year for NASCAR. I didn't see quarterback Tom Brady (New England Patriots) or Eli Manning (New York Giants) chatting with fans on game day. In addition to the unscripted access to the sports stars, my hot pass allowed me to literally go anywhere—even the racetrack itself.

It was uncomfortably exciting having unlimited access, and at times I worried about getting in the crew's way. Needless to say, I was in the middle of the action and got to experience firsthand what makes NASCAR such a fascinating sport.

Are you seeing a familiar thread here?

Personal access is the entry point for growing any brand.

Here's why.

Access Leads to Connection

Daytona fans were welcome to take part in defining the brand's signature event, and they did. For example, they were encouraged to sign the actual racetrack. They also mingled with the drivers and took pictures with them, had them sign something, or simply give them a jump high five.

You think a young fan who signed his name on the famous racetrack or had his picture taken with his favorite driver is ever going to forget the experience? He's a NASCAR lifer, just like your friend who met a Major Leaguer as a kid and still follows his team today even though he now lives in another city. Or just like that customer who received a personal message from the business owner and now won't spend her money elsewhere. Authentic access builds authentic connections between brands and fans. Loyalty comes along that path.

Connection Leads to Relationship

The incredible thing about NASCAR is that these brand-fan connection points create relationships with people of all ages. That's a nice-sized target. The key is to continue the conversation and deepen the relationship after the initial access was granted. This is something NASCAR wasn't doing much of when I attended the Daytona 500. My social media play-by-play updates to my own audience of 1.2 million served as a demonstration of what can happen on a much larger scale when an outsider like me or a loyal fan perpetuates the conversation about NASCAR over social media.

I didn't pull punches when it came to reporting about the experience. I went into it honestly. I told my audience I had no plans pretending to know the sport so I could come across as an expert. I simply promised they would experience the Daytona 500 through my rookie eyes, which might prove to be comical but nonetheless authentic. I used the #GiveNASCARaChance hashtag as a sort of motto for those in my audience who, like me, hadn't give the sport much thought before that day.

The hashtag alone ensured that my virtual play-by-play reached a much larger audience of true race fans who gladly joined in my education. As it turned out, I wasn't alone in my NASCAR phobia. The response I received from non-NASCAR fans who followed my Daytona 500 adventure was overwhelming. Many who thought they disliked NASCAR had, like me, just never given it a chance. After seeing behind-the-scenes photos, video, and other content from my time in Daytona, many decided to tune into the race for the first time.

Fans like this one, who had more than ten thousand followers at the time, were common:

 **Amy: Digital Royalty**
@AmyJoMartin

Josh Duhamel says hello. No big deal. This photo alone is enough for some to #GiveNascarAChance.
http://yfrog.com/h678olj

↩ Reply   ⇄ Retweet   ★ Favorite

20 Feb via Twitter for iPhone

 Elizabeth UFC
@FightGirlUFC

@AmyJoMartin vs. @DigitalRoyalty you're winning me over slowly. The photo was a big step.
http://yfrog.com/b678olj

↩ Reply   ⇄ Retweet   ★ Favorite

20 Feb via Twitter for iPhone

If even one of your followers had a Daytona experience with your brand and then did what I did, you'd be making good headway. But what if multiple people on a regular basis had a personal experience with your brand and then furthered the conversation over social media? What would that do for your brand?

Relationships Lead to Affinity

When like-minded people gather to enjoy a common experience, they tighten their bond for both one another and the experience itself. If you've ever been to any major sporting event like the Super Bowl or the World Series or the Daytona 500, you know that the experience bonded you to those around you. Even years later, if you met someone on a plane who attended the same event, the bond is there. There's something special about sharing an experience of that magnitude together, whether it's a sporting event or something else.

It's a good thing to win affinity from one individual, but it's a great thing when that individual has many others with whom to share the experience afterward. Social media makes this possible—incentivized follow-up surveys, not so much.

Affinity Leads to Influence

There's a reason so many sponsors are attracted to NASCAR: it has that rare but lucrative combination of a tightly knit but incredibly large community. That gives rise to the question: Who truly owns the NASCAR brand? Technically speaking, it's NASCAR. But practically speaking, both NASCAR and its loyal fans do. If NASCAR spends 364 days ignoring racing fans, how's the next year's Daytona 500 going to turn out?

Of course, the NASCAR brand wouldn't exist without the executives, teams, and drivers who make up the sport. In truth, what affinity creates is mutual influence. This is more obvious the larger the audience grows. The brand influences its audience to consider new products and embrace new paradigms. And the audience majority—the consensus—tells the brand what it values and what it does not. It reminds me of something else: a healthy relationship based on a foundation of trust.

Influence Leads to Conversion

The brand converts the fans to buyers with an increasing degree of loyalty. The more the brand continues to deliver the value the fans want, the more loyal (and lucrative) to the brand the audience becomes. This is why perpetuating the initial access you offer is so important.

Simultaneously, the fans use their influence to convert new followers to join the conversation and, eventually, the community. A case in point is that the NASCAR fans made a believer of me, a woman without a NASCAR bone in her body. NASCAR was a brand for which I had zero affinity. And then I met the fans of NASCAR, mingled with them, and experienced the sport—the brand—firsthand through their eyes. I had a blast, and I came to see what a loyal fan sees in the sport: not the full spectrum but certainly enough of it to move me from an ignorant outsider to an appreciative fan in a matter of one day. Am I crushing beer cans on my head or rocking a bikini top in the company of 150,000 of my closest friends? Not yet at least.

But I now have affinity for a sport I couldn't have cared less about before the experience. In the end, I was wrong about the NASCAR brand. And hundreds of others made the same admission. After having my mullet-laden misconceptions removed through access to the human side of NASCAR, I was left with a new understanding of the sport.

What if this sort of clarity and influence was available to your brand at any time simply because you provided access?

It is. You just need to be willing to accept the truth that you are not the only authority on your brand. The consensus is the authority on your brand too. Control freaks, this is where you dig deep.

What You Don't Know Can Hurt You

Yes, you brought your brand into the world—you gave it its first breath. But if you want people to love that brand and remain loyal, it has to be theirs too. They must own it with you. In the past, this allegedly happened through consistent quality. We came to love a brand we gained an affinity for and then came to learn we could count on it. We bought the same designer clothes or ate at the same restaurant or drove the same make of car because we liked the product and knew what to expect every time. Consistency of quality kept us loyal. But ultimately it was a surface loyalty that could be moved if the mood struck us right.

That's one way to go about brand loyalty. But it's not the best way now that you have a two-way conversation at your disposal.

Human personality is a much quicker and more effective way to differentiate your brand. And the more that people get to know your brand's human traits, the greater you are differentiated and the deeper their loyalty is rooted.

Brand ownership is not very deep when it's based only on surface traits like quality, aesthetics, and practicality. Social communication channels allow you to take your audience deeper so that their loyalty to your brand is rooted in human qualities that strengthen any relationship. And the best part about going deeper is that the relationship is owned by both parties. This mutual ownership—or mutual authority—is the key to lasting loyalty.

All relationships have their leading party and their following party. But the most successful ones learn to lean on each other's strengths and have equal value exchange. Your strength is innovation and the ability to respond—keeping your brand ahead of the curve and nimble enough to quickly change with the desire and needs of your other half. Your audience's strength is honesty and the ability to provide constant feedback—keeping your brand aware of the need to change, improve, or stay just the way it is. Show me a relationship with ongoing innovation and honesty, and I'll show you a relationship that has staying power. That's just as true on a one-to-one level as on a one-to-20-million.

The glue that holds loyal relationships together is listening. It is the two-way line that ensures that the benefits of innovation are passed on to your audience, and the benefits of honesty are passed on to you, your company, and the brand. However, this is where you must take the lead because what you don't know about your brand and its audience will eventually hurt you. Nobody wants to be irrelevant or blindsided.

Listening Louder

The first step to building consensus and benefiting from it is listening to your audience. You do this by asking questions that will inform the shaping or reshaping of your brand.

Many brands get caught in faux-improvement mode in which they, in an effort to mitigate risk, make only lateral movements. They aren't truly taking the brand to a higher level. They might change the color of a logo from mint green to kelly green or add a new flavor to the menu. What's the net of lateral movements that are generally based on market research a brand has paid someone else to tally? Consistency, such brands would say. But if you look up *consistency* in Webster, you'll find one of its synonyms is *monotony*.

Disruption is not always a bad thing. It's to be expected when you're innovating or wanting to stand out. The sea on sameness is a terrible place to be because you don't really know anything is wrong until you're already sunk. If you're listening properly, you'll know how to disrupt safely. Disruption isn't destruction: no harm has to be done in order to shake up a situation and garner the attention of audiences.

It's one thing to be reliable and deliver a consistent level of quality people can come to expect. Do that, and do it well. But don't let that be the basis or hallmark of your relationship with fans. You can go deeper. Even consistency gets old when's it's the only benefit.

Begin the listening cycle by asking questions that will protect your brand from remaining in a superficial relationship with its fans.

Once you've asked once and listened, engage them and listen again. You have already asked your audience questions that will initiate ways to improve your brand, and you listened to their answers. Now it's time to engage your audience with clarifying questions. One way to do this is to gather the information you've received from your initial round of listening, report the findings to your audience, and ask for confirmation or further clarification.

Shannon Lee, my friend and Bruce Lee's daughter, told me her father used to say, "Listen to the voices of the people around you. Listen to the fans—what

LISTENING CYCLE

they want and what they respond to. Any system or organization that ignores the need of the individual will at some point become static. It's all about the individual experience." Shannon is using social media to bridge her father's powerful legacy from the past with the future: "My father's legacy is so inspiring to many people, and social media allows me to keep that inspiration alive. We want people to question things and join the journey versus being passive. Inspiration is an emotionally fueled response to something. Everything begins with listening."

After I asked Phoenix Suns fans if they'd attend the tweet-up and purchase a ticket, I proceeded to ask them to help me plan the details of the evening:

When I was in my next meeting with the Suns executives (the ones who would say "a what-up?" when I mentioned a tweet-up), I showed them the real-time responses on my laptop as a way of proving we had enough fan support to make money off the idea.

Needless to say, we held the first ever professional sports tweet-up.

The evening went like this:

At 4:00 P.M., approximately 150 Suns Twitter followers who purchased special discounted game tickets met at Majerle's Sports Grill (named after former Suns star Dan Majerle) for appetizer and drinks specials. It was like a blind date, and I was the host connecting people and introducing them by their Twitter handles.

At 5:00 P.M., the same fans walked a couple of blocks to the US Airways Center, where we gave each of them a custom Suns T-shirt designed by the fans themselves and then escorted them to floor-side seats we had reserved for them to watch players warm up before the doors to the arena opened to the public. Exclusive access was a benefit they had asked for.

At approximately 6:30 P.M., the fans gathered outside the arena at the Bud Light Paseo stage to watch the live pregame TV broadcast in which I was interviewed about the tweet-up.

At 7:00 P.M., the fans were escorted to a special reserved section to watch the game. They were recognized throughout the game from the PA and on the Jumbotron screen above center court.

At approximately 9:30 P.M., the game concluded, and this select group of fans was escorted to the Suns' practice court for a live Q&A with the team's president of basketball operations and general manager at the time, five-time NBA champion Steve Kerr.

An hour later, the fans assembled for a group photo with Kerr. That's when they got their biggest and best surprise. Quietly, Shaquille had slipped onto the practice court. He didn't go unnoticed for long: soon the crowd erupted in cheers and Shaquille approached them, giving jump high fives, shaking hands, signing autographs, and taking pictures with anyone who asked. The night concluded with one final group photo with Shaquille in the middle of the tweet-up crowd who'd been treated to not only a special night with their favorite team and two of its premier stars; they'd been ushered behind the Suns' brand curtain where relationships with the human side of the brand were formed. The night was a huge success that made a big impact on loyal fans and initiated mutual influence between them and the Suns that the fans still tweet me about to this day.

Greg Esposito, then the senior content director for Fanster, sang praises of the tweet-up: "I'm thoroughly impressed with the PR staff. They rolled out the red carpet for a bunch of fans, and this event was one of the most impressive things I've ever seen a sports organization do." (A funny side note is that Shaquille was interviewed by ESPN the following day, and they asked him, "Can you explain what Twitter is?").

That was of course, only the beginning for the Suns. In the same way, your first listen, engage, listen again, and measure is only the inaugural launch of a continuous cycle. Perhaps the operative words are "Refine and Repeat."

As you initiate and then continue in the listening cycle, it becomes easier to keep a close eye on the growing sentiment and loyalty of your following. With each revolution of the cycle, you can refine your brand's message and meaning, which leads to greater influence with your followers and a more deeply rooted fan loyalty. The process starts out as experimentation—risky, yes—but eventually the experimentation turns into best practices. This, and not paying an external market research firm, is how you find your brand's sweet spot. Any other method of refining your brand results in an approximation at best. Only ongoing social media engagement allows you to truly remove the guesswork in branding.

I recently gave a keynote address to the employees at the MasterCard Worldwide Headquarters as a kickoff to its Social Jam 2012 and the unveiling of the MasterCard Global Conversation Suite. The Conversation Suite is a set of tools, technology, and savvy social people who enable the company to listen, engage, and converse in forty-three countries and twenty-six languages in real time across social media networks, blogs, and forums. Before the presentation, Andrew Bowins, MasterCard Worldwide's senior vice president of external communications, and I discussed the power of listening and overlap between social media and company culture. He proceeded to tell me about an employee named Kim, from the corporate finance department, who approached her boss inquiring if she could spend a dedicated amount of time each week to learn about social media and use the platform to listen to consumers, merchants, and industry observers in real time to learn more about what they care about and think of the company. Her boss approved.

Can you imagine how a company could transform itself if everyone within the organization spent time listening to customers firsthand? It may not seem intuitive for someone from finance to benefit from this strategy, but social communication tools have an impact on every aspect of a business. It's amazing what can be learned when we listen louder.

Engagement Rules Without Rules

The great news for noncreative types is that the sky is still the limit for the how-to of engagement. The renegade brands are still writing the rules. Actor and filmmaker Edward Burns is a good example.

We talked recently, and he explained how he has taken to Twitter in the past couple of years to engage his consensus in conversations about what songs should accompany certain parts of his films or what names certain characters should have. He's even asked followers for their ideas on how a story plot should unfold. The kicker is that he's not just asking the questions for the sake of asking. He actually takes the good advice and applies it. He's a renegade writing new rules for the art and science of filmmaking.

I applied a similar listening strategy with the title of this book. I tweeted a photo of the title typed on the first page of an early copy of the manuscript. I imagined it felt something like sharing a photo of a new baby. Then I listened to feedback. I was humbled by the number and caliber of people who responded:

Amy: Digital Royalty
@AmyJoMartin

Thoughts on my working book title? Scary step, like
sharing a potential baby name:
instagr.am/p/G65vzkkHF_/

Guns N' Roses
@gunsnroses

@AmyJoMartin @DigitalRoyalty Nice! Sounds like
something new to break :) #WhatRules
#TeamRenegades

Amy: Digital Royalty
@AmyJoMartin

@jonmchu Glad you like the title, Jon. I'm sharing your
tweet in a meeting w/my editor/publisher tomorrow.
Screenshot. Boom. Thank you!

Jon Chu
@jonchu

@AmyJoMartin I love the Chapter Zero Part too. That
made me smile.

Amy: Digital Royalty
@AmyJoMartin

Spoke w/my publisher. Official title of our book:
Renegades Write the Rules. Thanks
#TeamRenegades! on.fb.me/wxmZpG

Asking my followers for feedback on the title developed a quick consensus on whether it was good, just so-so, or horrible. That was the honesty of my audience working for me and giving me a greater sense of confidence in sending this book out into the marketplace. But what asking my followers for book title feedback also did was give them access to join me in the innovation process. While many of my followers and I go way back to 2008, this still served as a great way to deepen their loyalty to a new aspect of my brand—the book. Before this new product hit bookstore shelves, I had already verified affinity for its title and initiated a greater sense of ownership in a large portion of my book-reading audience. For all of you who helped name this baby, thank you!

How would you like to know your fans' affinity for a certain product before you spent money to develop, market, or sell it? And how would you like to deepen your fans' loyalty before the product hit stores or the service was offered? I don't know what your R&D budget is, but if it doesn't include a social media listening strategy, you're missing your best opportunity to research, test, market, retest, and sell your brand's offerings.

I talk to many executives and entrepreneurs who fear jumping fully into the space because of the time it will take up every day and the learning curve they will have to overcome for it to make them money. The irony is that social media can save you more money with a smaller investment of time than any risk-mitigating R&D expense you can undertake. Most businesses spend millions trying to figure out what products are working and what ones should come next when they could simply embrace social media, build a following of loyal fans, and ask them. I know more than one renegade brand that has done what I just described for next to nothing.

Let me give you an example of one who recently (and admittedly) came to his senses.

Simon Cowell is a man at the forefront of pop culture and someone I've admired for years. He's one of the best talent scouts of our time, responsible for discovering acts from Kelly Clarkson to One Direction, who recently made history by becoming the first British group to debut at number 1 on the Billboard Top 200. Cowell is also a prime-time hit machine credited with favorite TV shows in the United States and United Kingdom. He's also known as a fashion icon, making the grayscale V-neck a simple, timeless staple.

Yet while Cowell makes his living staying ahead of the mainstream curve, he recently confessed he was behind with social media. In fact, he had declared it wasn't personally for him.

In the first season of FOX's *The X Factor* USA, the blockbuster show Cowell brought to the United States on the heels of its enormous success in the United Kingdom, Cowell's team hired Digital Royalty to set up real-time social media metrics for the show. This was also when he decided to take the Twitter leap himself.

Now, Cowell insists he "can't imagine doing the show without social media." What changed his mind?

He gave three reasons that provide a summary of why the consensus is the true authority on your brand today (if you let it be):

1. *Ease and detail of research.* "It's the best market research in the world," he asserted, "and it's quick." My team provides real-time analysis of *The X Factor's* social conversation to Cowell, as well as in-depth analysis of each episode after the show that allows the cast, crew, and talent to make changes as soon as the next show. This information has also heavily influenced the shaping of the upcoming seasons, including changes they hadn't intended to make but became necessary through the frequency of certain conversations.

2. *Instantaneous feedback.* "I instantly know if someone likes something," he explained, "or, more importantly, hates something." Television ratings take time. Advertising, sponsorship, and product placement results and analyses also take time. But social media's instantaneous feedback allows all *The X Factor* USA stakeholders to constantly read the current temperature of viewership, engagement, and sentiment. This is invaluable information for avoiding major setbacks that would otherwise show up in only falling Nielsen ratings that give no indicator of why a certain percentage of people are no longer watching the show. With social media, Simon and his associates can read what people are saying and immediately peg the

culprit. And if it's still not obvious through the current conversations of viewers, Cowell can open up a new conversation and directly ask viewers what they didn't like. This isn't rocket science, after all.

3. *Quick remedies.* We've been here before with Shaquille's retirement announcement. With social media, influencers like Simon Cowell can avoid spin, bias, and fallacy by delivering news directly to their audience. Twitter even has a verification system in place—a "verified" check mark appears next to the authentic Twitter account—that ensures followers of a major celebrity or corporate brand that the news coming from certain accounts is from the person it says it's from. The phony accounts vying for free publicity or aiming to harm your brand are easier to expose this way. For example, when several cast-change rumors began to spread during the first season of the show over mainstream media and other Twitter accounts, Simon used his account to deliver messages and personal videos that cleared up any confusion or false information. "You can remedy something with a tweet," he said. And he's right. But a level of trust must already exist in order for your stream of information to be believed. You can't just hop on social media and "create a viral campaign" to clean up an extramarital mess, for instance.

So far so good for *The X Factor* USA and Cowell. There hasn't been a problem they couldn't quickly remedy, and with the level of trust now firmly established between fans and the show's brand, I suspect this trend will continue. Like a lasting relationship, they will thrive on each other's strengths.

The beauty of embracing social media today is that it's not nearly as risky as it once was. In fact, it's now without a doubt riskier to remain on the outside. While early adopters had the advantage of winning over the masses because the space was less crowded, late adopters have the advantage of streamlining their success based on the lessons of those before them. This book is an example, and I hope it has given you a lot more confidence in this new area.

A few years ago, I remember meeting with Tom Jolly, at the time the sports editor at the *New York Times*. I met him over Twitter, of course, because he spent a great deal of time on Twitter sharing sports news and his personal opinions. That is what initially caught my eye—I felt that I was getting to know a human behind that stark masthead.

At the time, the *New York Times* believed social media could be what would keep the paper relevant. They understood social media could offer real-time news that couldn't wait for the newspaper the following morning. He gave me a tour of the *Times* building, and it was as if the old school had just discovered the future. The transition was literally happening as we walked the halls, and Tom explained that they frequently had late-night meetings trying to decide if they would tweet certain news instead of letting the Web site or paper get it first. I showed Tom how to post video to his Twitter account, and he'd ride into New York on the train and record videos. The *New York Times* was one of the first major media outlets to have a robust list of journalists on Twitter. They gave them the power to report over social media, and it paid off.

The brands that built their influence within the world of social media early on are now seeing the return on their investment. But the truth is that while early adopters are years ahead in their entrance into the space, if you learn from their successes and mistakes, you can reap rewards much more quickly than they did. They had to weather years of public hesitance before the general public widely embraced social media. Certainly establishing trust with your brand's consensus is foundational to monetizing social media, but you no longer need years to begin seeing a return. In fact, some brands are reaping the rewards immediately.

The X Factor was a good example from the entertainment industry. But for my business leaders, DoubleTree by Hilton provides an inspiring example.

Last year Digital Royalty spent several weeks with thousands of DoubleTree by Hilton executives and employees, strategizing ways to engage their audience in order to innovate customer service and deepen customer loyalty. Our initial strategy, which the company continues today, began with a tweet in which DoubleTree by Hilton asked followers to click a link to tell them #LittleThings they could do to improve their travel experience.

DoubleTree by Hilton
@doubletree

Tell us what #LittleThings could improve your travel experience for a chance to win: on.fb.me/yhE6m2

↩ Reply   ⟲ Retweet   ★ Favorite

The link took customers to DoubleTree by Hilton's Facebook page, where they were asked to like the page to complete the survey.

Once a follower finished the survey, the Facebook page immediately generated a thank-you message that included a live tweet stream of the #LittleThings hashtag that not only gave a subtle nod to the community that was being deepened but also invited customers to join in the conversation with their own tweet about one of their #LittleThings that would make a big difference in their travel experience.

This was a win on two fronts. The offering not only generated valuable feedback to help the DoubleTree by Hilton brand customize its service offerings. It also generated social media conversation about the brand on the two big channels, Twitter and Facebook.

The mix of valuable feedback for the brand and a sweet prize for guests, as well as heightened awareness of both, resulted in exponential growth in DoubleTree by Hilton's online community. In only ten days following the campaign's launch, the brand's Facebook likes had already grown by more than 30 percent. Its Twitter following had increased by more than 15 percent. And its weekly "People Talking About This" metric, the brand's Facebook engagement measurement, had increased by more than 427 percent.

Perhaps the biggest win of all is that social channels, unlike traditional channels, provide a communication bridge that doesn't have a shelf life. The fan dialogue never turns off as long as your brand is willing to continue engaging it and using what is learned in the conversation to add value when, where, and how fans want it.

You can't go up to someone at a cocktail party whom you've never met before and ask this person to buy a time share (although I fear a lot of businesses still ask their sales force to do precisely this). The same rules apply to social media.

The one rule renegades can't rewrite is the rule of trust. It cannot be bought. It cannot be sold. It cannot be finagled through false promises that end up as a bunch of hype or fancy facades that don't have any humanity behind them.

Trust must be earned through good old-fashioned give-and-take over time. And then trust must be strengthened through a deeper and constant understanding of the other party's needs and desires. How else will you keep them happy if not by making it your job to always know what they want? That's another way of saying that if you don't trust in the authority of your brand's consensus, you won't earn its trust.

Intense passion and fierce work ethic are two silver bullets that renegades share. Whether it's on the court or through his foundation, I've followed Steve Nash's renegade ways since my days with the Phoenix Suns. Nash, a point guard, is often referred to as one of the hardest-working athletes who has ever played the game. When it comes to innovation, Steve recently told me that he doesn't care how good the idea is. "It comes down to the person behind the idea, their work ethic, passion, charisma and energy," he said. "In order to innovate, you have to invest heavily, whether it's financial investment or giving everything you have to it. We're all innovators in our own way. We create the way we get through life, on a day-to-day basis."

You might have a blockbuster idea that can help your fans better than they now realize. But if you don't entrust it to their premarket opinion, you're putting a great idea in grave danger.

131

The way innovation works best today is not the way it has always worked. Yes, you can still initiate the idea. And when you do, ask for forgiveness after the fact rather than permission before the fact. Yes, you can still introduce the idea to the world, and yes, there will be times when the world won't be ready for your idea. But this isn't the Middle Ages. Great ideas find an audience, even when the naysayers are powerful. Right, Egypt and Libya? Put your idea out there, and if it's big and it's right, it will stick.

And if it sticks, it's worth more than media attention. If you humanize your brand through social media in the way I've discussed to this point, social media is absolutely monetizable. I know you've been waiting for this. Don't forget that I'm a business owner in the end. I understand that what matters for any brand when the social media dust settles is the bottom line.

You want returns?

Let me hear you say, "Show me the money!"

Or just turn the page.

RULE 7

There's a New ROI in Town

Innovation Allergy: *New Metrics*

I would be lying if I said it was a divinely inspired event. The truth is that necessity was the catalyst for invention. Facebook was just catching on, and Twitter was still a baby. I was prepping for a meeting where I hoped to convince a major consumer products and goods (CPG) brand that my celebrity client was more influential in social media than other celebrities. Therefore, my case concluded, they should invest their dollars in my proposed social media endorsement deal. The dilemma was the metrics.

I knew this big company would expect me to defend my client's value with the standard cold metrics: reach, frequency, page views, impressions, eyeballs captured, and so on. Executives who are about to spend lots of money like numbers, even when they know they're flawed. Numbers help justify decisions, remove some risk, and mitigate accountability. But they can also keep a great opportunity from being fully considered. Heidi Burgett, a Nike PR renegade, once reminded me that Einstein said it this way: "Not everything that counts can be counted. Not everything that can be counted, counts."

I recently had a discussion with Rob Palleschi, global head of DoubleTree by Hilton, on the topic of monetizing social media. He said, "Social media is another method of communication, and in the scheme of things what does it really cost? The cost is negligible. I don't focus so much on return on investment. I see social media as necessary distribution channels that we need to engage with. The more we put in, the more we'll get out. The more we engage in the social space, the more we build relationships with travelers, and the more we're going to get their loyalty. Additionally, the more they'll tell us what they like or what they don't like."

Rob has a personal Twitter account and speaks directly to guests and media on behalf of the brand. He confessed, "Once I started doing it, it took relationships to a completely different level. Traditional marketing doesn't suffice anymore; our brand is about delivering experiences. Without a doubt, I'm a renegade. Tell me no, and then I'm going to do it. Usually there's a disclaimer and an attorney nearby too."

I agreed with the company's executives that cold metrics held some value, but I insisted they were no longer enough. I explained that my celebrity client could have the same number or even fewer fans, followers, and page views as another celebrity but still be a better investment. How? Influence. If my client could convert more followers into something valuable like click-throughs, sign-ups, media consumption, or product purchases, then my client was worth more than others. Impressions rarely convert, I said, but influence rarely doesn't. They eventually saw the light, and we began what would be a profitable relationship for both my client's brand and theirs. But not every branding meeting has such a happy ending.

In truth, five years later, I still have the same conversation. I'm still in prove-it mode more often than not. While receptivity to the new metrics has improved, the improvement is less than you might think.

Here's why that's the case.

Warm metrics—engagement levels, viral factors, and sentiment analysis—don't exactly leave people warm and fuzzy. The phrase itself is a bit ironic. The warm data I present just aren't as comforting as traditional cold metrics because they defy easy math. "How do you assign a value to sentiment?" is a common question I hear. It seems too subjective. The truth, however, is that it's more objective than cold metrics.

For instance, data showing that twenty of one hundred customers communicated the same problem with their shoes is far more conclusive (not to mention useful) than data that merely show twenty of one hundred customers returned their shoes. Would you rather know how to fix a product flaw and save future sales? Or know only the number of returns per one hundred sales and try to figure a way to bring the number down? There's a lot you can do with a regular influx of that sort of information, especially when you know it's not contrived.

The unspoken issue with traditional cold metrics is that at times, we are so dead set on justifying an investment that we search until we find the metrics that support our decision. That tendency is cleverly spoofed by a series of Geico commercials where a gentleman stands next to a table offering a "car insurance taste test." On the table are two cups of juice: sample A and sample B. He asks a passerby to take the test, drinking one sample and then the other. Without fail, sample A is "delicious" and "refreshing," and sample B is "disgusting" and "terrible." The gentleman tester then reveals that sample A was the Geico sample and sample B was "Other" insurance company. Obviously the taste of juice has nothing to do with car insurance, let alone Geico's quality of insurance. But the ad makes a good point: sometimes we'll try anything to prove our brand's worth. Geico hopes you'll also see the satire.

With social media, you now have access to the sorts of information that in years past could have kept top brands from slipping and kept floundering brands from falling off the map. Blended with the traditional metrics, warm metrics give a clearer picture of what an audience thinks of your offerings and what specifically attracts them to your brand in the first place. With this clarity, you can move more nimbly to meet demands, identify difficulties, and fuel loyalty.

At the time I was meeting with the major CPG brand, most companies were downright dismissive of warm metrics. They were the fluffy intangibles you pointed to when you couldn't build a statistical case for investment. Business purists had (and often still have) a love affair with structure: long-standing rules, industry standards, and traditional case studies where solid numbers win the day. A love affair with sentiment? Not so much.

I was recently having lunch with Andy White, a partner in the VegasTechFund. He's constantly being pitched ideas and evaluating them. He said that one of the primary challenges with vetting an opportunity is that many businesses make up research to validate their direction, their product, or their success in general. I agreed. We are so anxious to measure things and prove we're right that we don't measure correctly or with the right intent. To be successful, we have to listen to our audience and be willing to be wrong, learn from that understanding, make adjustments, and listen again. It should be acceptable to fail; there's innocent intent in failure if you failed trying to meet a need. Andy agreed.

I still believed in this blend of cold and warm metrics. I knew that if you ignored the warm metrics, you ran the risk of missing your quickest path to returns because cold metrics alone are an unsound way to gauge a brand's level of influence with consumers. And influence was the ultimate measurement, whether you were a celebrity pitching awareness or a company launching a new product line. Low influence equals lower conversion; high influence equals higher conversion—no matter what measuring stick you use.

If you ignored the cold metrics, you're doing yourself a major disservice because that's your reach. You need reach to be influential; otherwise you're on an island by yourself. Also, it's safe to say that the majority of corporate marketers and media buyers need to justify their spend with impressions somewhere in the equation. The point is that you need both hot and cold.

On one of my 210 flights one year, I was determined to show this in a way that executives could appreciate. On a Southwest Airlines napkin, I first doodled what I called the new ROI. Instead of standing for "return on investment," purely a dollars-in, dollars-out measurement, this new ROI stands for "return on influence," a measurement that combines the cold metrics traditionalists love (total number of fans and followers—or the number of impressions) with the warm metrics only social communication channels provide (engagement, affinity and sentiment). This is how we measure the new ROI:

COLD METRICS   WARM METRICS

ROI
RETURN ON INFLUENCE

This form of measurement has since evolved and been customized for brands based on their needs and the metrics that are most important to them. However, it was very foreign to me when I introduced the concept of mixing warm and cold metrics. Fortunately, I had a small arsenal of successes to draw on. In my position with the Suns, for instance, I had to continually prove fan affinity to big brand-marketing partners who spent seven figures on their sponsorship deals with the team. These brands were big names so they had options, often with other sports teams in the National Football League, National Hockey League, and Major League Baseball, and more traditional channels like TV spots that might be able to tell a better cold metric story than I could. But my time with the Suns had taught me that social media provides a way to measure fan affinity that a TV spot never could.

How?

Social media communication is two-way. It's a dialogue versus the monologue of traditional marketing campaigns. Instead of merely creating short-term buzz, social media creates conversations, sometimes unprompted conversations that can be listened to, recorded, and measured. With a history of such conversations at my side, no longer did I have to say, "Trust me, our fans really like the team." I had the hard data to prove that fans really liked us.

Once you recognize that each entry into an online conversation is generating influence, you track it. A Facebook like is a transaction. An @ reply to a tweet is a transaction. So is a retweet. So is a purchase that results from a retweet or a like. Unlike, say, traditional TV advertising, marketers can now track online behavior from a social channel from the initial message all the way through to purchase—and they can score each message with an influence metric (ROI). And as you know by now, the majority of these messages aren't sales pitches. Some of the best-performing tweets—like Shaquille's ice cream photo and Dana White's verbal beat down—do so well because they are classic personifications of the brand. Followers can retweet them and say, in effect, "This is exactly what I love about him."

If you ask Shaquille O'Neal what his number one goal in life is, he'll say, "To make people laugh." That's his true intent, and it's how he lives his life. By humanizing his own brand and showing people the Shaquille (person) behind the Shaq (persona), he's built a loyal relationship with his fans, which has allowed him to monetize his social influence. He's been interviewed on this subject. This is the formula he uses when allocating his time on social media channels:

- 70% Make 'em laugh
- 20% Inspire 'em
- 10% Sell 'em something

Yep, 10 percent of the time he's trying to sell you something but he's able to do that only because he's earned that 10 percent based on the pure intent to humor and inspire 90 percent of the time—which started as 100 percent of the time. He's the first to admit he's going to talk about certain products from time to time, but he won't do it if he doesn't genuinely believe in the product. And more than likely, he'll be entertaining you when he's socially pitching you anyway. The net is that his 10 percent equates to touch points of natural brand integration versus interruption.

Many brands I work with have their highest ROI scores following messages you couldn't have planned if you had a creative meeting every hour for a week. Who could have brainstormed that Shaquille O'Neal, arguably the greatest center of the modern era, would get more action from a tweet of himself eating an ice cream cone than of him dunking a basketball or digging on Kobe or D-Wade? Such is the nature of social media because such is human nature. Sometimes you can't predict what people will gravitate to; you can only be ready when they do. Social media keeps you connected so that you can best capitalize on spikes in activity, as when Dana White accidentally tweeted his phone number and then took fans' calls—and then started taking fans' calls on a regular basis.

How do you run with a spike in attention, from, say, an online sale? Get people's e-mail addresses and send out a creative follow-up blast? Good luck with that. What you need to do is continue the conversation, continue to offer values, and follow through to conversion.

The next step to using your new ROI score is to link your influence to investment. This is where the dollars come back in. If you divide the total revenue generated by a social media message or campaign by the number of social media fans and followers, you get a revenue per fan and follower (RevPAF) value:

RevPAF
REVENUE PER AVAILABLE FAN AND FOLLOWER

This is the metric that opens eyes. When you can see that the per-head value of each fan has increased on the basis of a social media strategy, monetizing your brand becomes straightforward: remain engaged in ways your fans value and come up with innovative ways to bump them up the loyalty ladder.

The main benefit to the RevPAF metric is that your level of investment in branding efforts becomes simplified. The beauty of social media is that once you've established an online presence on Twitter or Facebook (preferably both),

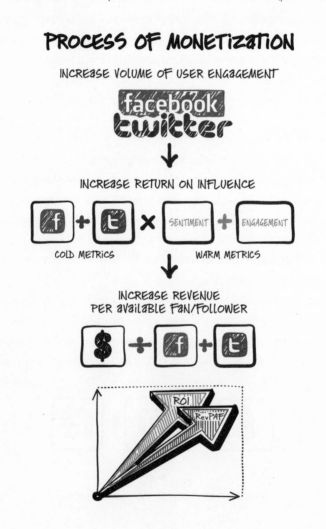

maintaining your relationship with fans and followers is a minimal expense—often it's free—when compared to traditional marketing budgets that are high-dollar hits or misses. The whole process of humanizing your brand to monetize it looks like this:

I've found with brands varying from DoubleTree by Hilton to high-profile individuals that there is a direct correlation between return on influence (new ROI) and RevPAF. As you become more influential (ROI goes up), the dollar value of each fan and follower goes up (RevPAF goes up). The same goes for a decreasing ROI.

The more that marketers accept the concept of measuring influence relative to reach, the more quickly social media industry standards will surface. Social networking revolves around the art of people interacting with people, not logos. Remember that people have influence. Things like logos, products, and taglines do not. Ultimately influence is the power that differentiates one brand from another, especially at the top where things like customer service, product quality, and price point are relatively equal.

> As a kid, I loved numbers. I would count everything. How many times I was placed in time-out, how many seconds it took to get out, how many times I popped a bubble, how many steps on the way home from school, how many miles I water-skied behind the boat. In college, numbers were easy. I would take calculus I, II, or III over any class that made me read a book and write about what I had just read. Too much gray area. How would I know if what I was writing was correct? Numbers were black and white, very much like my personality. All or nothing. No gray areas in my mind. Zilch. I tend to do something 100 percent or not at all, which I've learned can quickly turn my best assets into my biggest liabilities. Like you, perhaps, I had to unlearn my dependence on black and white numbers and learn a gray renegade way of measuring the things that really mattered—a way of counting the things that cannot be counted.

Humanize to Monetize

In a similar way that advertising titan Leo Burnett found success personifying brands with mascots like Tony the Tiger, the Pillsbury Doughboy, and the Jolly Green Giant, today's renegade businesses invite consumers to look behind the logo to the humans who embody their brand. While many companies shy away from this idea because it's new and without two decades of proven research, some use intuition and take a more daring approach.

Monte Carlo Resort and Casino in Las Vegas is a great example. It has humanized its brand by giving customers unscripted access to key players in the company. Among them are president and CEO Anton Nikodemus, vice president of marketing Jessica Cipolla-Tario, and executive director of casino marketing Johnny Quinn. All use Twitter to do more than tout their brand and offer value to consumers; they also show off the personality behind the hotel through banter with followers and each other.

Last year, we helped the three executives launch a groundbreaking social media competition in which each one created a Monte Carlo package deal that included their favorite indulgences and gave it the same name as their Twitter handles: a battle royal to be promoted solely through social media. The competition was developed to increase social media engagement, increase awareness about the property's value offering, and convert potential guests into actual guests.

While the deals spoke for themselves—with perks ranging from room specials to discounted dinners and show tickets to spa packages—the real fun came from the personality behind each package and the banter among them.

Did you see yourself as a member of #TeamJohnny, hanging with the Jabbawockeez entertainment show and buying rounds of drinks for friends?

Or did you see yourself as a player on #TeamPrez, indulging in steak dinners and a lavish VIP status?

Or how about being the star of #TeamDiva, treating yourself to the ultimate spa experiences?

There was something for everyone, and once Monte Carlo guests heard about the rivalry, it was hard not to join the fun and root for a team. Our metrics clearly showed engagement ramped up. From there, the friendly competition between executives was nonstop.

Anton Nikodemus
@MonteCarloPrez

@MonteCarloVegas let the competition begin. Which package do u REALLY want! The Presidential package rocks! bit.ly/MCPrez Johnny who?

↩ Reply   ⇄ Retweet   ★ Favorite

7 Jun via Twitter for iPhone

Jessica
@MonteCarloDiva

I declare today #TeamDIVA day! Last day to get on board @MonteCarloVegas Diva style bit.ly/MCDiva #Team DIVA #Team DIVA #Team DIVA

↩ Reply   ⇄ Retweet   ★ Favorite

8:03 AM - 29 Jun 11 via Twitter for iPhone - Embed this Tweet

Monte Carlo Casino
@MonteCarloVegas

@TeamJOHNNY is in the lead (http://bit.lyMCJohnny) @JohnnyLasVegas. Where you at #TeamDIVA @MonteCarloDiva and #TeamPREZ @MonteCarloPrez?

↩ Reply   ⇄ Retweet   ★ Favorite

They talked trash, called each other names, and challenged one another to dance-offs. It was not only a blast for guests to follow and engage; the executives ate it up too. The strategy took joy on the job to a whole new level. More important, the big resort and casino was bridging the virtual and physical worlds, ushering customers behind the brightly lit signs, fancy amenities, and manicured grounds and into the living rooms of three of its top executives. The result? Since implementing the strategy, Monte Carlo Resort and Casino has nearly doubled its revenue per available fan and follower (RevPAF). Money doesn't lie.

Through social media, Monte Carlo was—and still is—conveying that a stay at the property is not just a purchase; it's the beginning of a relationship with a brand they hope you'll enjoy and find value in for a long time.

We tracked revenue for each executive package, and while we eventually revealed which executive's team won the most bookings (conversion), I can say that in the end, the Monte Carlo brand was the real winner. Increased brand awareness led to increased engagement. As engagement increased, brand sentiment also increased, which led to increased revenue. All this from that "crazy social media fad."

In addition to revenue and outward-facing benefits, the internal corporate culture benefited. The fact that the top executives were publicly embracing social media and showing their true personalities was a sign to all employees that the company was taking this new form of communication seriously—so seriously that they had dedicated portions of their days to this initiative. Also, it sent the internal team the memo that the executives were people who liked to have fun and were willing to get comfortable with being uncomfortable. That's the start of a culture shift that pays big dividends.

This so-called fad is not just for crazies anymore. Then again, maybe that's precisely who it's for. But ultimately you're crazier not to embrace it—just the wrong kind of crazier.

A Compounding Effect

Your company may not have a Tony the Tiger or Jolly Green Giant, but your brand's CEO or president or executive vice president may follow after charismatic social media powerhouses like Tony Hsieh of Zappos and Richard Branson of the Virgin Group, who have become pillars of brand recognition and customer relations. Whether you really show up to the social media space or not, the fact is that people are going to talk about your brand. You might as well show up with a plan, a purpose, and a personality to lead the discussion and add a face to your brand's name. If yours is a corporate brand, the good news is that this new ROI extends its returns beyond the company's bottom line.

Essentially the brand that becomes humanized often fuels the creation of an individual brand for the person who humanized it. Drinks on you! There are plenty of examples. Hsieh and Branson have both had huge individual success writing books and speaking, among other things. But you don't have to run a multibillion-dollar company to reap this benefit. I saw this happen with Digital Royalty.

While I am the primary face of my company's brand, the ROI of the Digital Royalty brand creates a market for Amy Jo Martin, the individual. For three years I have had many pay-per-tweet companies approach me. It's never been something I've subscribed to as a sound philosophy for brand marketers or talent for a variety of fairly obvious reasons. None of our talent brands have participated in pay-per-tweet programs either. The insincerity factor is hard to get around.

But last year I was approached with a different sort of opportunity. Chevrolet had the idea to launch a Web series in which I interviewed and interacted with athletes from various sports around the country. When Chevy approached me about the endorsement, I quickly realized they get it. They wanted to help me provide unique value to my own audience (who they hoped would like them too) in the form of unexpected sports content. I was just the vehicle for delivering the value in an authentic way while driving a Chevy Cruze. The sequence of events in considering the opportunity went like this:

Act 1
- *Chevy to me:* Check out the car. Did I like it? This was a must because I'm a horrible liar.
- Check. Like the car.

Act 2

- *Me to Chevy:* Wait, so Chevy is going to pay me to basically do what I love (sports and social media) and additionally give me a car?

- Check. Exactly.

Act 3

- *Me to Chevy:* Did I have to change anything about what I'm currently doing and the content I'm currently providing via social media?

- No. Not at all. Just please refrain from talking about our competition.

The details from there were simple: a new car and a six-figure payout over a three-month period for a specific number of Web videos in which I would attend epic sporting events and chat with the athletes themselves or the players behind the players (such as trainers, coaches, or agents) and provide my audience exclusive access into the unexpected side of sports.

No brainer. Already did that. Deal.

Typically my celebrity clients are the ones in front of the camera, so this was a whole new thing for me. At the very least, I knew my followers would get a good laugh at my expense. (I hoped not *that* big.) But in the end, nothing changed. I was myself and told my audience up front what I was doing. We enjoyed the ride together.

This is an important distinction of the new ROI. If I am a brand followers already know and respect, I don't have to put on an act or a costume—a veneered identity—in order to introduce something to them. I've earned their trust. I don't have to do any persuading.

Chevy came to me because they knew I already had influence with my followers that I'd earned by being me and delivering to them value they'd made clear they wanted. When it was time to carry out my end of the endorsement deal, did I spam my followers with Chevy Cruze ads or poorly veiled social media content? Absolutely not. I delivered exclusive content to them that they'd already made clear they valued. I just happened to be driving a Chevy Cruze while doing it. Score for both of us.

Now if only we could package that goodwill and scale it globally. Oh wait. We can. And some brands already are.

Amy: Digital Royalty
@AmyJoMartin

I parked my car in the middle of @MLB's Tampa Bay Rays left field. Video: http:bit.ly/gFwcEL #cruzearati @RaysBaseball

↩ Reply   ⟲ Retweet   ★ Favorite

RULE 8

The Act of Good Can Be Scaled

Innovation Allergy: *Self-Sacrifice*

Something very common happened to me in 2010 on US Airways Flight 544 from Vancouver to Phoenix. But what happened afterward is something truly uncommon.

I left my very beloved iPad at seat 15A. It was more than a gadget many people would love to get their hands on: mine also contained a lot of sensitive information. That is when I went from a simple customer to a customer who needed service.

In a state of panic and with a tinge of hope, I sent this tweet:

Amy: Digital Royalty
@AmyJoMartin

Please help, @USAirways! Left my iPad in seat 15A on flight 544 - Vancouver to Phoenix. Plane is headed to DFW now :(

↩ Reply   ⇄ Retweet   ★ Favorite

3:10 PM - 13 June 10 via Web

Tweeting to US Airways just might get me my iPad back. After all, as a loyal Southwest Airlines customer and follower, I've seen customer service in action using Twitter. In fact, @SouthwestAir was actively assisting customers throughout the day on that Sunday. When I looked up what @USAirways had been up to, my hopes fell even more. No one had sent a tweet in four days, and the last time anyone responded to a customer who needed service was five days earlier.

Fortunately, US Airways wasn't my only hope. Suddenly my phone started blowing up with tweet replies from hundreds of my followers who were responding to my virtual distress signal. Some were sending me phone numbers to US Airways and to airports' customer service departments. Others offered advice on how to get it back. Kind friends from Dallas (where the plane was headed next) volunteered to drive to the airport to retrieve my iPad, and dozens of others reached out to the @USAirways account on my behalf.

At that point I felt like a lucky woman with so much support. Then in the middle of this outpouring of generosity came my tweet-in-shining-armor under the handle: @This_JustIn. And this Justin saved the day. He'd made a couple of phone calls on my behalf, reaching out to a contact he had at the airline. Next thing I knew, he tweeted me with great news: my iPad would be riding with the captain on a return flight to Phoenix, where we would be happily (and gratefully) reunited.

A few hours later, I returned to the airport and picked up the iPad. The captain personally escorted it off the plane and delivered it into my hands.

There are many lessons to take from this story. For one, don't leave your unlocked iPad on a plane. (It's now password-protected.) But the most valuable lesson surrounds the power of humans helping humans.

Thanks to social media, there are huge opportunities for titans of industry such as US Airways to humanize their brand in a humanitarian way. Imagine if @USAirways was listening around the clock (since, ahem, they *fly* around the clock) instead of listening only during regular business hours as they say. They would not only have had an opportunity to give amazing customer service to a passenger but also to do it in front of thousands of people who were listening through social media. Through my following alone, people were literally rooting for them to succeed. They, however, were too busy doing business as usual.

Otherwise this would have been an easy win. They had a simple tool that allowed them to reply immediately, remedy the situation, and be heroes while thousands followed along. They also had a captain flying the plane who cared enough about his passengers to temporarily take custody of my iPad and personally return it to me. But, alas, they weren't actively engaged in listening to their customers. They had tickets to print, bags to check, and planes to fly. And so @This_JustIn_ became the hero instead.

Sure, the pilot was the secondary hero, but I bet that if US Airways executives are reading this, it's the first time they've heard the story. The pilot's help had nothing to do with the brand for which he worked. He was just one person given an opportunity to help another, and I'd fly a plane he flew anytime. But it wouldn't matter one bit whether it was a US Airways plane.

Times have changed, my metal-winged friends. The brand no longer determines when or where they want customers to communicate. This is especially true of big brands like airlines that are always open for business somewhere in the world. Today, deciding not to embrace social media is like deciding to ditch the phone. Imagine if US Airways decided the phone wasn't relevant and stopped answering it for five days. They wouldn't do that, of course. But they essentially did.

The needs of your audience exist whether or not you acknowledge and address them in a timely fashion. The strongest brands that build the highest degree of loyalty have their ears to the ground every minute through social media and can jump to serve or solve problems the minute their name is called.

Am I being too hard on US Airways? Is business far more complicated than I understand?

Virgin Airlines doesn't think so. "Virgin America was built to be social," writes *Forbes* columnist Mark Fidelman. "The customer acquisition strategy is social. Their teammates [Virgin's term for employees] are social. Their Executives are social and Virgin Companies are social . . . Virgin America is a young airline, but an experienced airline. They don't act their age; they act as if they are decades more experienced."[1]

What is this experience worth? The highest positive consumer sentiment, 80 percent, of any U.S. airline.[2] Want to know who holds the second highest positive sentiment score? My hometown favorite, Southwest Airlines, at 76 percent. For the record, Virgin America and Southwest also score highest (4 out of 5 and 5 out of 5, respectively) on the Glassdoor Employee Satisfaction Index and the Trip Advisor Traveler Rating (96%, which is tied with JetBlue, and 97%, respectively). It is no coincidence that Virgin America (as well as Virgin Atlantic) and Southwest Airlines have the most robust, respected social media strategies in the airline industry.

It is no longer feasible to insist that social media is just a fad or that it's not necessary. It's also not enough to insist you'll "eventually do it." Social media is not only the future of business; it is this moment of business as well. And the more moments you miss, the more irrelevant you will become. To opt out of social media is an irresponsible business decision. It's quickly becoming a fatal business decision.

The Business of Humanity

What brands like Virgin and Southwest understand is that social media is ultimately the bridge that permanently links business ventures and humanitarian ones, making "doing business" and "doing good" one and the same.

Doing good for your local community or the world at large is nothing new for brands, but such ventures have historically been add-ons that had little, if any, bearing on the bottom line. That is no longer the case.

You probably noticed that over the past five to ten years, there has been an upswing in businesses attempting to modernize their brand by linking it to a national charity, cause, or foundation. For a time, being green became necessary, so brands added that to their bio, so to speak. Then being conscious of unfair and unethical overseas labor became necessary to add on. Again, they added it to the "About" section of their Web site.

While such add-ons are certainly positive steps for any business and, without a doubt, for humanity in general, they have largely been like pieces of jewelry on prom night—mere accessories to help brands look the part and remain relevant.

While I think it's safe to say we all applaud the upswing in humanitarianism, it can be quite alarming when any brand that is careful in its About section and includes the necessary humanitarian accessories remains careless about its greatest and most constant opportunity for doing good, spreading cheer, and acting ethically: its daily interactions with fans, followers, and customers.

In this sense, social media is the great humanitarian measuring stick. They are every brand's accountability, and the public callout that goes something like this: "If you say you care, you will listen, remain engaged, and constantly strive for stronger relationships with your audience."

This takes more than a product special on Facebook once a month. It takes more than inspirational quotes on Twitter every other day. It takes the humans behind your brand engaging the humans in front of your brand in ways that make your general business strategy about adding as much value to as many people as often as possible. Renegade brands know that the best kind of value transcends the transactional realm and enters the space where real lives are improved in little ways and sometimes in very big ways. Renegade brands also know that nothing makes this more possible than social media.

When the National Hockey League's Los Angeles Kings asked Digital Royalty to help them better engage fans on a regular basis, we figured we'd start with a bang to show fans the true hearts of the Kings franchise and players who for years had been very involved in local charities. We conceived and implemented the first-ever NHL Hashtag Battle between the Kings and the Colorado Avalanche. For every #GoKings or #GoAvs hashtag that was tweeted, the corresponding team would donate one dollar to Children's Hospital Los Angeles or the Kroenke Sports Charities as part of the NHL's month-long Hockey Fights Cancer campaign.

We ultimately wanted to get #GoKings in front of more than just hockey fans because we knew NHL fans weren't the only people who cared about these charities. Our goal was to reach the general sports fan and the Saturday night tweeter who was looking to tweet for the greater good. But like any other business endeavor, reaching our goals was not without challenges.

For starters, the Kings-Avs game wasn't nationally televised. It therefore wasn't easily accessible to the average sports fan. On top of that, it was a Saturday during college football season, and the epic Ultimate Fighting Championship 121 heavyweight event was also taking place in the same target market (Los Angeles). Oh, and did I mention that the San Francisco Giants were trying to win the National League Pennant against the Philadelphia Phillies and that game started within minutes of the Kings game?

We looked at all the other sporting events—and let's be honest, there were bigger events on every level—positively. They provided us a larger captive sports audience to tap into based solely on their broadcast reach. We knew a healthy percentage of the Twitter population would be communicating heavily about sports. But would they be tweeting about the Kings versus Avs game? We needed to influence a few key groups in order to make it happen and raise some money for these important charities:

1. *Kings and Avs fans.* These teams have an intense rivalry, and we wanted to translate it into a social competition. With bragging rights on the line, we trusted that the tweets would come pouring in. They did. Check.

2. *NHL fans.* The support of the NHL helped get the word out about the battle to hockey fans who may not have been closely following the Kings or the Avalanche. This Coyotes fan is a perfect example. Check.

3. *Online influencers.* We targeted specific sports influencers who helped us get the battle into the pathways of their followers. Baseball fan and actress Alyssa Milano tweeted about the battle as well as the Los Angeles Galaxy soccer team. LIVESTRONG CEO Doug Ulman (a pioneer at using social

media for the greater good) also supported our mission, as did Sarah Palin. We had several million followers paying attention. Check.

SarahPalin
@Sarah PalinUSA

#GoKings! Please tweet #GoKings. For every #GoKings tweeted up till 12am ET, $1 goes to LA Children's Hospital!

◀ Reply   🔁 Retweet   ★ Favorite

**7 minues ago via web
Retweeted by 100+ others**

4. *The charitable-minded.* We anticipated that once the influencers got involved, #GoKings and #GoAvs would be reaching the eyes of people who would participate solely to help raise money for the higher objective. We knew this had worked when we started seeing "I'm not a hockey fan but . . ." tweets. Check.

Once the puck dropped, the chain reaction of support kicked in immediately. By the end of the first period, approximately twenty minutes later, #GoKings had shot to the number one worldwide trending topic. That status added welcome fuel to the fire, and the tweets kept pouring in from hockey fans and nonhockey fans alike. By the end of the game, the official hashtag score was #GoKings 29,374 and #GoAvs 13,876.

In less than two hours, through a simple social media strategy at a hockey game, we turned two sports businesses into something bigger and raised more than forty-three thousand dollars for cancer. Not lost in this success is the fact that both the Kings and the Avs added thousands of Twitter and Facebook fans to their fold and another layer of depth to their brands in the process. Doing good does good for your business as well.

Imagine if this sort of result reached a grander scale, with thousands, if not millions, of brands taking on a similar mind-set and strategy. What could we accomplish?

Today we're starting to see a sneak peak of what social media can become. Renegade brands are forging the trail.

Delivering a Bigger Kind of Value

Word-of-mouth is nothing new, and it's still the most powerful form of marketing. However, when brands identify and listen to their natural evangelists to help shape and activate their passion, word-of-mouth becomes an epic force—or should I say, "word of thumb." Case in point is Zappos.com CEO Tony Hsieh.

When I first met Tony, I was working for the Suns, and the HR department had about had enough of me. I had recruited fifteen to twenty people in the front office to join Twitter, including the mascot. Human resources insisted we had a social media policy in place. There is often this mix of hesitance and a desire for structure in many corporate minds when it comes to letting social media become a companywide strategy. I understand this from many standpoints. No business wants to jump into any full-scale change recklessly, and social media is no exception. (By the way, this book should mitigate the recklessness.)

I did some research and found one company that had overtly embraced Twitter and encouraged its employees to tweet on behalf of the company as themselves: Zappos.com, known at that time as the online shoe retailer. In an effort to offer my HR department an example of the social media policy passed down from a respected executive of a blockbuster brand, I shot Tony Hsieh, who followed me, a direct message question about the Zappos policy.

Hi Tony, I head up digital media at the Phoenix Suns. Do you mind sharing the Zappos social media policy? Thanks! Amy Jo

I knew Zappos was a renegade in this space: it had given customer service representatives and executives freedom to respond to and serve customers in real time. There didn't seem to be a vetting process for what they could and could not do—or at least one that took more than about a minute—so I could clearly see that Tony had a solid handle on how his company used social media. I also knew my hesitant HR department would consider him a highly credible source.

Tony direct-messaged me back two weeks later:

Be real and use your best judgement.

I loved reading his words, which are actually written into the Zappos employee manual (I've since learned that "Be real and use your best judgment" is the entire Zappos communication policy.) I also knew this policy would not settle the nerves of some in front offices who were riding the social media fence mainly because they were waiting for a way to embrace it and still maintain full control. Zappos' policy would be a catalyst to some and a harsh reality to others. But in both cases, the words lit the path to big branding success today.

The biggest hurdle to full-scale implementation of social media is the issue of control. Many business executives fear what might happen if employees have too much freedom. They frequently tighten their grip on company culture and regularly suffocate the life out of it. Guess what? The customers can tell.

The great irony is that employees—especially customer service representatives and salespeople—are the primary daily touch points between your brand and your audience. By position alone, they will regularly influence your brand's ability to serve and add value to your audience. They will also affect the perception of your brand for better or worse because suffocated employees don't usually make good impressions on customers.

Even if you are the primary face of the brand—even if you've managed to humanize your brand through your social media presence—if your teammates in your business aren't able to deliver on what you promise, you are just another elaborate gimmick. Your brand has a veneer called @you that looks nice but is only hiding a cheaply constructed company.

The flip side is that when the leader of a brand puts himself or herself out there and becomes the human behind the brand, and then backs that relational offering up with additional human interactions that support and add to who he or she is, the brand's roots multiply and grow deeper. From the strength of this foundation, a major movement can occur—one that is far bigger and more purposeful than merely boosting your core business numbers. It will boost your bottom line too in the most organic and sustainable way possible.

Here's what I mean.

After Tony's direct message reply, he and I exchanged a couple of more messages before agreeing to meet at an event the following month. As fellow renegades, we hit it off right away. That led to, among other things, Digital Royalty working with Tony and his Zappos teammates on the marketing strategy for his first book: *Delivering Happiness: A Path to Profits, Passion and Purpose*.[3] The book itself served as an extension of what the Zappos brand had already established with customers, which had led to $1 billion in gross merchandise sales annually and a regular spot on *Fortune* magazine's annual "Best Companies to Work For" list.

As part of the *Delivering Happiness* book team, we helped organize the Very Happy Person (VHP) program to harness the power of Tony's most active, vocal, and passionate supporters. The goal? To fuel a happiness movement that would live beyond the successful launch of the book and the successful foundation of the brand.

To begin, the Digital Royalty team developed and implemented a cross-platform social media campaign to deliver worldwide happiness leading up to the launch of the book. The strategy was to make use of the organic nature of social media to not only generate exposure for the book, but create a dialogue everyone could be a part of no matter where in the world they were located. The movement was less about encouraging people to purchase the book and more about creating a conversation and subsequent movement that people would gravitate to because of the value it offered. We trusted that those who were truly affected would happily buy the book.

Here are the specific components of the campaign. Notice that each one is focused first on the higher objective of the message behind the movement and then on selling a book.

Livestream Events

For eight weeks, we hosted a series of Delivering Happiness Virtual Happy Hours from a different city each week. The happy hour was broadcast live on the Delivering Happiness Ustream.TV and Justin.tv channels and was focused on one central theme–happiness. And so the Happy Hours featured such things as a baby kangaroo, drinking dice, and awkward-but-enthusiastic kara-oke, to name a few. Tony, Jenn Lim (his coauthor), and I hosted a variety of guests during these live streams, from epic skater Tony Hawk to groundbreak-ing entrepreneur Gary Vaynerchuk. It was a kickback happy hour environment with talk show style every Friday afternoon. Viewers and fans of the movement would tune in from all over the world and ask us questions using Facebook, Twitter, and Ustream.TV social stream.

In the end, Delivering Happiness Virtual Happy Hours were viewed by more than 300,000 people from around the globe, and those viewers consumed 340,000 minutes of Tony and the Zappos brand delivering happiness. Wouldn't it be nice to have your brand's best moments broadcast for the world to see? Nothing is stopping you but the courage to show some skin, get comfortable being uncomfortable, and be your own media channel. Sometimes you are your brand's biggest hurdle. But you are also its biggest hero if you are willing.

Very Happy People Program

No matter what their platform or page traffic, several hundred bloggers were encouraged to apply on the Delivering Happiness Web site to become part of the Very Happy People Program. One thing that was unique about this blogger program is that it wasn't limited to business bloggers. The program included everyone from food bloggers to photography bloggers. By not limiting it to a specific industry or topic, our strategy was able to reach a larger and more diverse audience. Everyone likes happiness, after all. My team's self-named "Blogger Relations Department" (comprising every member of the team) dug through hundreds of blogs to identify bloggers who fit within the VHP program requirements.

Each blogger who was selected received two advance copies of the book—one to keep and one to give away to their own audience. In return, we simply asked each blogger to write an honest blog post or review of the book during the week of the launch.

By the time *Delivering Happiness* was launched, there were approximately eight hundred bloggers in the Blogger Program who helped promote and review the book. Approximately half fulfilled all their responsibilities.

Facebook

Facebook was leveraged to encourage interaction among fans, as well as encourage those who had advance copies of *Delivering Happiness* to post photos of their Happy Place on the Facebook wall, whether that was on the beach or from their own backyard. Two winners were selected for their photo

160

submissions and announced on the day of launch. One winner's photo was from the sandy beaches of San Sebastian, Spain, and the other was with his college-ruled spiral notebook. Both won a free autographed copy of the book and a Delivering Happiness T-shirt.

We received photo submissions from all over the world in the three weeks prior to the official launch of the book. The contest built such a strong momentum that the Facebook page dedicated to the book promotion continues to receive photos from fans and followers to this day, despite the content officially ending the day the book launched.

Twitter

The Delivering Happiness team partnered with the LIVESTRONG crew and set a goal to raise $33,333 by the launch of the book on June 7, 2010. Leveraging Twitter, we encouraged followers to join the Delivering Happiness and LIVESTRONG movement by making three promotional pushes leading up to the launch party. A base of more than 5 million Twitter followers was created by pooling influential tweeters such as @LanceArmstrong, @Zappos, @LIVESTRONGCEO, and @AmyJoMartin, among others.

Our combined crews did better than we hoped. We raised $50,000 to help support the LIVESTRONG organization. Just as important, we let current Zappos followers and would-be followers know that the brand was bigger than business as usual.

I dare say this win on many fronts wouldn't have been so successful without the renegade approach to business that both Tony Hsieh and Doug Ulman apply daily. I recently talked to Doug, and he shared some great insights into this combination of doing good and doing good business. He said, "One lesson that we've learned and the way that adversity has affected us is that when you engage in these social media tools, you open yourselves up to criticism and controversy. Everyone has a voice. How we've dealt with it has been a learning experience. It isn't a bad thing; I actually think it's good. From an advocacy perspective, if you're not making some people upset, you're not advocating strong enough. How you react and overcome that is different. [LIVESTRONG] is audacious and sometimes naive, and we stretch the boundaries and try new things all in the name of spreading health and healing in greater ways on bigger scales. We know that if we don't keep trying and take risks, we can't get anywhere worth going."

Meetup Everywhere and Sponsored Meetup Book Clubs

Meetup.com's Meetup Everywhere platform allows like-minded people from around the world to organize groups and events in their own community. To celebrate the launch of the *Delivering Happiness* book, people were encouraged to organize a Delivering Happiness Meetup group and join the Delivering Happiness team on June 7, 2010, to watch the livestream coverage of the launch party in New York City. Each group was sent complimentary copies of the book so that their groups could chat about the book and everything happy. This spawned one hundred book clubs across the country on meetup.com, giving the Delivering Happiness team regular access to more than forty-three thousand people.

The 133 Delivering Happiness Meetup groups joined the movement and hosted events from locations around the world, including Ireland, Malaysia, and Peru. Each group then tuned in to live coverage of the launch party in New York City via livestream.

The result of all this delivering happiness? The day the book launched, it was ranked number 1 on Amazon and Barnes & Noble. One week later, it was number 1 on the *New York Times* best-seller list. Not bad for a renegade author who'd never written a book before and a bunch of social media renegades who had never launched a book before. And according to the plan, the party didn't end there.

After the book launch, the Delivering Happiness team members hit the road for three months in a giant tour bus. The goal was simple: continue the spread of happiness throughout the country and, as a constant reminder, deliver the books to keep the party going in workplaces around the world after the bus left.

While a brand disengaged with its audience will find that few show up when there is something to celebrate, an engaged brand throws a good party, especially when the celebration is for something everyone received. The Swedish proverb rings all the more true in the social media sphere: "Friendship doubles our joy and divides our grief."

Social media democratizes access. Traditional gatekeepers and physical boundaries have lost their power to a network where brands and ideas are granted global access if they deliver widespread, transcendent value. This sort of value is much bigger than a satisfactory purchase. Now is the time to stretch your notion of business as usual. Or maybe you just take Richard Branson's approach and say, "Screw business as usual."[4]

Personally I like the second take.

I was speaking at an event in Chicago and was invited along with Doug Ulman, Shane Battier, and other keynote speakers to attend a kick-off event for Chicago Ideas Week, hosted at the Mayor of Chicago's house. Prior to the event, Alana, from my team, made an e-mail intro-duction between me and Robert Fogarty, the founder of Dear World, whom she had met at an event in New Orleans during Tony Hsieh's *Delivering Happiness* book tour. I quickly spotted Robert out of the crowd, standing with his camera and writing on a person's arm with what appeared to be a black sharpie. This instantly reminded me of Tony Hsieh's affinity for writing smiley faces on people's hands with sharpies.

Robert and I had the opportunity to connect while he was taking my photograph, and I was instantly inspired by his contagious passion for his work. Dear World, which was once called Dear New Orleans, was a social movement inspired by Hurricane Katrina. Robert photo-graphed personal notes of support and love that were shared with those affected by the devastating hurricane. After practicing exhaust-ing resilience and persistence, his concept and message are catching on, and now Dear World is a global movement that has evolved to unite all people through a series of short, meaningful messages, whether of love, hope, fear, or inspiration. His powerful photos are meant to help change the way we view the world.

Resourcing the World to Improve the World

The greater the volume of water, the higher the waves can climb and the greater the splash can be. Today's renegades are no longer lone rangers. They are individual risk takers, yes, but they find the greatest resources available to them in risking more intimate relationships with people they both know and don't know, believing in a greater power from collaboration than isolation, and possessing enough strength and leadership to trade their egos for a grander notion of whatever it is they are most passionate about: happiness, justice, service, financial freedom. The ceiling on the renegade is limited only by imagination, conversation, and humility. The biggest victories are always "us" and "we," not "I" and "me."

This truth became all the more real to me through two recent, unexpectedly connected events.

First, rewind to the earthquake and tsunami in Japan in 2011, a crisis that unfolded moment by moment over Twitter. I was on the treadmill watching CNN when the news came across the traditional media wires. Pictures of the tragedy—of people fighting for their lives and of buildings, cars, and debris rushing in flooded coastal towns—were flashing on and off the screen. And then the major news outlet cut to something about Charlie Sheen's most recent brouhaha. Apparently ratings were more important in that moment. Millions couldn't have disagreed more.

I pulled up Twitter on my iPad and watched the streams of tweet traffic. While mainstream media outlets featured photos of Hollywood's latest disaster, I was amazed to see everyone's typical Twitter activities pushed aside for this disaster that was far more critical. Within minutes, the global social media community was in the business of helping humanity. The revelation was personally epic—one of the moments of my life with the greatest impact. People wanted to help, and help was a click away. Just as a small community bands together in the face of local devastation, Twitter brought the global community together. The focus of literally millions of people became helping by disseminating valuable information and instantly donating money to aid organizations like the Red Cross that were already on their way to the area of the disaster.

While nature's wrath was devastating so many lives, altruism formed its own tsunami of help and healing through social media. I jumped in head first and offered up my following of 1.2 million as a resource to get the word out to affected areas and other immediate areas like Hawaii, where the potential of more damage was very possible. I wasn't doing anything different from any other concerned global citizen that evening. We were all helping as fast as we could and as far as we could reach.

Immediately replies started flooding in offering links I could share and requesting resources from those in my following and beyond. I stayed up the entire night answering these replies and trying to get the word out to as many

Amy:Digital Royalty
@AmyJoMartin

Call friends/family in Hawaii & wake them up. RT @itendtotalkalot Pacific Tsunami Warning just elevated. Major risk. 1.usa.gov/giYDSX

↰ Reply   ⤾ Retweet   ★ Favorite

11 May via web

Amy:Digital Royalty
@AmyJoMartin

RT @tokyoreporter If you're trying to call people in Tokyo, Japan use (03) numbers. Mobile networks still down #tsunami

↰ Reply   ⤾ Retweet   ★ Favorite

11 May via web

people in harm's way and as many people willing to help as possible. It was a night I will never forget. A greater sense of purpose had been integrated seamlessly into a world I was already passionate about.

A few months later, the world watched the Women's World Cup Final between this recently devastated country of Japan and the United States. It was a record-setting night for Twitter when, at one point, 7,196 tweets per second were sent, the most in its short history and much higher than the tweet rate on the night Osama bin Laden's death was announced or during the latest Super Bowl.

Why was women's soccer, historically an overlooked sport, the source of this record-breaking tweet rate? Popularity? Nope. The Super Bowl was more popular from the standpoint of number of viewers. Most traditional media coverage? Not that either. Bin Laden's death had more.

The record-breaking engagement was the result of something less business-like. The world had recently watched Japan experience an enormous tragedy. And Team USA had just played some dramatic earlier games that had exposed some of the vibrant players' personalities. The brands of both teams had been humanized. We all felt an emotional connection. We were engaged on a deeper level with the women behind the two brands on the field.

I had the privilege of attending the Women's World Cup Final in Germany thanks to my friend at Nike, Heidi Burgett. Sitting fieldside, I was able to expose what television feeds couldn't, and the content resonated. But analytics showed that nothing outperformed a photo I tweeted of Team Japan thanking the world for their support after the devastating tsunami. Not even live video of the crowd as goals were scored and exclusive behind-the-scenes photos performed as well.

Not only did the world audience want to see Japan celebrate and feel good, they wanted to join in that feeling, so they participated in a record-breaking fashion. This wasn't about soccer, sports, or patriotism. This was about live emotion, feeling good, and sharing the feeling. That evening, good went viral, and the value of the teams' brands rose significantly. People want to help,

want to be caught up in something bigger than themselves, and want to share the adventure with others.

Consider what this would mean to a large enterprise that embraced social media throughout every division of the company. Community relations and charitable initiatives would gain wider exposure and quicker momentum. They would also go a much longer way to creating an admired brand identity.

While it is difficult to measure the impact that scaling acts of goodness will have on company culture, one thing is certain: every brand has an opportunity to motivate every person along the value chain to add purpose to their days in a way that is unmatched historically.

In the end, every brand leaves a person a little better or a little worse with every interaction. From your splash page to your customer service representatives' first response to the first tweet you and your teammates send each day, there is no such thing as a neutral interface. Who you are and why you do what you do every minute of every day will leave your audience a little better or a little worse. The brands that matter today and tomorrow are the ones that have embraced the simplest and most authentic way to ensure that people are far more often better for interacting with them.

Power is rapidly shifting to the hands (or should we say fingers?) of the masses, and it's trending positive. Renegades embrace that power and lead it into a force for scaling goodness and good business and then sharing the benefits with humanity.

How far will this go? Further than I'm sure any of us can imagine right now. But some renegade will. And then the rules will be elevated again.

Renegades, keep writing the rules.

The Next Chapter

Innovation Allergy: *The Unknown*

A while back, I was at an upscale client event making small talk, which I'm secretly allergic to, and a gentleman approached me. He proceeded to use fancy words to describe his fancy job and his important and influential friends. Two-and-a-half strikes for this fancy fellow.

One of the words he used was *orthogonal*. Little did he know how much impact that word has had on every aspect of my life. I pretended to be interested in his uh mazing word, which he continued to discuss as if the definition was obvious. With eyes glazing over, I deduced it would be awkward to ask Suri to define *orthogonal* mid-monologue, so I sneakily checked my trusty dictionary app instead: "Orthogonal: Intersecting or lying at right angles, a matrix which preserves length or distance."

Ahhh. I had previously blogged about something I called the "intersection of innovation," demonstrating that true bliss resides where a person's passion, skill, and purpose collide. Suddenly this blissful intersection had a new name: "orthogonal bliss." I have since simplified the term to "Royal Bliss." Much more fitting.

Your ongoing innovation revolves around this orthogonal intersection of your passion, your skill, and your purpose in life. The more you focus on opportunities that call on your sharpest skills and strongest passions in order to produce a result that fulfills your purpose, the more bliss you will have in your days. It looks like this:

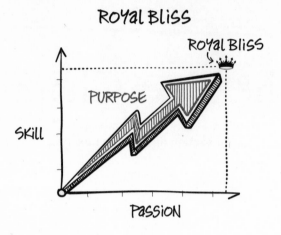

This notion of intersecting things we aren't used to goes beyond personal bliss. When you intersect things that haven't been mixed before, new possibilities arise in your life, your business endeavors, and the world too. Within those new possibilities are new solutions to longstanding problems and new opportunities that can reshape outdated protocols.

One warning: when you choose to intersect things that have not been mixed before, you must expect adversity. This adversity doesn't change your responsibility as an innovator to inspire others to see the value in your new mixture so they come to embrace the mixture with their own skill, passion, and purpose, and then share it with others. It is the eternal obligation of renegades to collide with nonrenegades and recruit them to a better way. Not everyone will go along at first as the traditional audience fears and fights the disruptive, abnormal collision. But if the mixture is blissful, acceptance will eventually occur, and you'll have diffusion of innovation.

These new communication channels called social media are ultimately about innovating the way we do business. This intersection of business and social media creates discomfort. But it is a blissful discomfort if you will pour your sharpest skills, strongest passions, and highest purposes into the mix.

Did you know that people who understand their purpose live an average of seven years longer than people who don't?

 # Ruthann Jensen
@BlackHillsDiva

Know your purpose. People who know why they wake up in the morning live up to seven years longer than those who don't.

Mom knows best, right? The statistic is more than a vote of confidence from my mom. Where skill, passion, and purpose collide, bliss resides, and this is not just my opinion. MetLife and Blue Zones Power conducted a study that showed people who wake up with a sense of purpose live up to seven years longer than those who don't.[1]

This place of ideal intersection is also where work is no longer work. For the longest time, I had an excess of skill and passion yet a deficit of purpose. My life arrow wasn't heading north. I was like the orthogonal diagram without the arrow. I would jump back and forth between what I was good at and what I was passionate about. Sometimes I'd have both going at the same time, but they weren't going in any purposeful direction other than building a business.

That's when I met Simon Sinek, who taught me that if I wasn't starting with my "Why?" I was bound for trouble.

I've since learned to make sure my work is always in integrity with my purpose. It's one thing to put in twenty-hour days for months at a time and build a successful company that rewards me financially. It's an entirely better thing when that hard work creates a successful business that also rewards me spiritually.

Today I'm writing the rules for my next chapter and injecting a higher purpose in everything I do. That begins with expanding the communities I've been building online through social media channels for the past several years. It's now time to bridge the virtual and physical worlds and build an innovation community in the physical world.

The most community-minded city in the world is being built right now in downtown Las Vegas thanks to the vision of Zappos.com CEO Tony Hsieh who believes, "If we fix the cities, we fix the world." He envisioned and is funding a $350 million project to revitalize downtown Las Vegas and turn it into a hub of thoughtful, innovative, and globally minded businesses that change the world one city at a time. Digital Royalty has partnered with Tony, and we have just moved our headquarters to downtown Las Vegas to be part of this groundbreaking innovation. This is Tony and me exchanging a Skype high five to officially close our deal one Saturday afternoon.

Digital Royalty has also partnered with the NBA's Baron Davis, point guard for the New York Knicks. I met Baron several years ago during the NBA All-Star Game in Phoenix when I worked for the Phoenix Suns. The league's

commissioner, David Stern, hosted an annual NBA Tech Summit in town a few days before the game. Not just anyone can get into the NBA Tech Summit. If you're not the CEO of a major brand, you're not getting in the door.

Going to this summit was a dream of mine, so I decided to volunteer at the check-in desk and try to sneak inside after the games began. Turns out that Baron Davis, NBA player/nerd, without a Tech Summit invitation, also planned to crash the digital Disneyland. We met outside the Tech Summit, and I helped Baron set up a twitter account for his infamous beard from the hallway because I wasn't allowed inside after all. (Baron was allowed in; I was not.) We have been good friends ever since. Baron has always been an early adopter of social platforms with the ability to spot growth potential early on. Today he's our investor and was our intern at Digital Royalty this summer in downtown Las Vegas.

In my next chapter, Digital Royalty will set out to redefine innovation through education. One of the primary reasons I wrote this book was that I believe in the power of sharing personal stories because it accelerates the process of learning on any level and in any industry. But there's a need for each of us to relearn the way we learn. Education goes beyond classes and curriculum. Through simple storytelling, we can humanize the way we learn, making it more enjoyable and more applicable. So share your stories; share your lessons. Let's speed up the process of learning, and teach each other how to innovate the way we lead our lives, businesses, communities, countries, and, ultimately, world. Digital Royalty University is launching a Buy One, Give One program. We call this reverse BOGO. For each hour (or module) of education purchased through Digital Royalty University online, we will be giving an hour of education back to individuals and foundations who are unable to purchase the education for themselves.

But that's only my innovative idea. What more could be accomplished if we all innovated on a regular basis! Social media makes it possible.

As you begin your own renegade journey of innovation, make sure you're in integrity with yourself and following what I refer to as your life compass—the

LIFE COMPASS

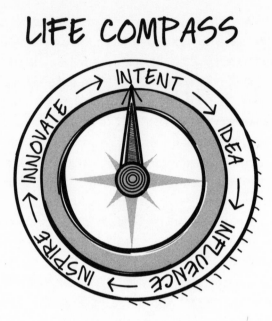

critical ingredients that if incorporated in order inevitably lead to innovation: intent, idea, influence, and inspiration.

Begin your days with your intent (your why). That's your life's arrow of integrity that ensures you are moving in the direction of your purpose. Your intentions set the stage for the rest of the innovation process and determine how your idea gains influence and whether it inspires others. With your intent defined, you then need an idea. From intent and idea, you must then gain influence for your idea in order to make it more scalable and reach more people. Once it gains influence, your audience then determines whether it inspires them enough to embrace it. You've not truly innovated until an audience embraces your idea—and that audience needs to be bigger than your mom and dad. Yes, it's risky to toss any idea to the crowd, but it's the only way to measure your idea's true worth. And if it's worthy, the rewards will come, and they will open doors for your next idea.

Follow the compass again and again, and soon your life will gain revolutionary momentum. Embrace the pull. Trust the revolution. Innovate your life.

As it turns out, you can have it all. You just have to define what your "all" is and then accept that it is always evolving. Onward and upward.

APPENDIX A
Digital Royalty's Core Values

Together my team and I have crafted core values to help us improve our day and quality of life. They are the number one priority at Digital Royalty. We hire, fire, and select whom we partner with based on this list of core values. When implemented, they propel us toward a better day and quality of life because how we spend our days is how we spend our lives.

1. KEEP IT ROYAL

   Royal Renegades live by the Golden Rule: both sides of the relationship must be equal, with ongoing value exchange and reciprocation.

2. OWN IT

   Integrity, responsibility, and community. We take responsibility for our lives, our results, and what's greater than ourselves. We are responsible for writing the rules and living by them.

3. RENEGADES WRITE THE RULES

   We are innovation advocates who color outside the lines. Innovation allergies begone.

4. HOW WE SPEND OUR DAYS IS HOW WE SPEND OUR LIVES

   If we're not having fun and feeling free, we're doing something wrong. We design our own days.

5. TEAMWORK MAKES THE DREAM WORK

   We support ourselves, each other, and our clients. We inspire each other to be free to innovate our lives.

6. BE A SOCIAL ROCKET SCIENTIST

   Our mixture of measurement and creativity is our X factor. Magic happens when we combine numbers with an emotional connection.

7. PAUSE AND LISTEN

   Strive to become an expert listener in both the virtual and physical worlds.

8. EXERCISE THE MIND

   Practice learning something new each day and sharing it with one person (a team member, client, or partner).

9. INJECT ZANINESS

   We are committed to being the fun part of someone else's day. We do the unexpected.

APPENDIX B
Lessons Learned

'I've become a serious advocate for accelerating the process of learning and innovation. One way to expedite this process is to exchange lessons so others can leapfrog the mistakes. As a first-time entrepreneur, I became well aware of what I didn't know from the beginning. That self-awareness has a way of continuing to grow as your team, business, and vision grow. Here are a few lessons I wish I had known from the beginning.

1. Where passion, skill, and purpose collide, bliss resides.

2. Beware of the shiny object syndrome (SOS). It's important to know the difference between an opportunity and a distraction.

3. You can color outside the lines without crossing the line. Disruption and destruction have two different outcomes.

4. Learn how to push your own buttons. It's important to motivate and inspire yourself. Everyone else is busy.

5. The people you choose to do business with will be the most important decisions you make. Those you say no to are just as important as who you say yes to.

6. You can have it all; you just have to define what your "all" is and accept that it is always evolving.

7. A five-degree shift changes your entire trajectory.

8. Your hustle factor is often your differentiating factor. Work hard.

9. Design your own day because how we spend our days is how we spend our lives.

10. Learn to control your thoughts, and you will be free.

11. Take risks, experiment, and fail early. When everyone else hops on the bandwagon, their failing process begins as you begin to win. Then share your lessons with others.

12. Accelerate the process of learning by sharing your mistakes so others can leapfrog them and sharing your lessons so others can snag them for free.

13. People come into your life for a reason, a season, or a lifetime. Just be where your feet are, and enjoy the journey.

14. Don't forget the importance of your personal brand. Your personality, confidence, and the way you conduct yourself define your brand. You can always improve it.

15. Learn when to ask for forgiveness versus permission. Just make sure to bring your results with you.

Notes

0

1. Wikipedia: http://en.wikipedia.org/wiki/Innovation.
2. H. Leech, "Bono Backs Kony Video Campaign," *Sunday Times*, Mar. 11, 2012.
3. L. Carroll, *Alice in Wonderland* (1865).
4. Special thanks to Roy Williams of the Wizard Academy in Buda, Texas, for introducing these brainstorming insights in his *Monday Morning Memo*, Jan. 6, 2012, http://www.monday morningmemo.com/newsletters/read/1965.
5. J. Steinbeck, *East of Eden* (1952).
6. A. Osborn, *Applied Imagination* (New York: Scribner, 1953).
7. J. Lehrer, "Groupthink: The Brainstorming Myth," *New Yorker*, Jan. 30, 2012, http://www.new yorker.com/reporting/2012/01/30/120130fa_fact_lehrer?currentPage=all.

Rule 3

1. "Just 31 Percent Hold Favorable Opinion of Tiger Woods," *Rasmussen Reports*, Mar. 16, 2011, http://www.rasmussenreports.com/public_content/lifestyle/people/march_2011/just_31_ hold_favorable_opinion_of_tiger_woods.
2. From a time line of Gallup polls on Bill Clinton in the White House, found here: http://www .gallup.com/poll/116584/presidential-approval-ratings-bill-clinton.aspx.
3. J. Paolini, "Winning Isn't Everything—The Woods Brand," *AgencySpy*, Apr. 3, 2012, http://www .mediabistro.com/agencyspy/op-ed-winning-isnt-everything-the-tiger-woods-brand_b31379.
4. "Michelle Obama Outshines All Others in Favorability Poll," *Gallup Politics*, July 22, 2010, http:// www.gallup.com/poll/141524/Michelle-Obama-Outshines-Others-Favorability-Poll.aspx.

5. R. Lusetich, "Tiger Double-Bogeys Media Relations," *FOX Sports Digital*, May 1, 2012, http://msn.foxsports.com/golf/story/Tiger-Woods-misses-mark-with-video-QA-session-043012.

6. Paolini, "Winning Isn't Everything—The Woods Brand."

7. B. Kelley, "Tiger Woods Earnings: What Is Tiger's Annual Income?" *About.com Guide*, n.d., http://golf.about.com/od/tigerwoods/f/tiger-woods-earnings.htm.

8. *USA Today*, Dec. 2, 2010.http://www.usatoday.com/sports/golf/pga/2010–12–02-pga-tour-releases-schedule_N.htm.

9. Kelley, "Tiger Woods Earnings."

10. Many thanks to brilliant author Simon Sinek for making sense of this for me. Simon Sinek: "How Great Leaders Inspire Action," Sept. 2009, http://www.ted.com/talks/simon_sinek_how_great_leaders_inspire_action.html

11. J. Stein, "Love Me, Love My Brand, Says the Sultan of Snark," *Time*, May 24, 2010, http://www.time.com/time/magazine/article/0,9171,1989137,00.html.

12. R. Branson, *Screw Business as Usual* (New York: Portfolio, 2011), p. 7.

Rule 4

1. Although my friends at Twitter headquarters cannot technically share the statistics of celebrities with whom I don't work, they did verify that DJ clearly dominates in this area.

2. M. Bonchek, "How Top Brands Pull Customers into Orbit," Harvard Business Review Blog Network, Mar. 5, 2012, http://blogs.hbr.org/cs/2012/03/how_top_brands_pull_customers.html.

Rule 8

1. M. Fidelman, "The Secret to Virgin America's Social Business Success," *Seek Omega*, Sept. 29, 2011, http://www.seekomega.com/2011/09/the-secret-to-virgin-americas-social-business-success-infographic-comparison/.

2. According to Scout Labs, a trusted source for measuring consumer sentiment for brands.

3. T. Hsieh, *Delivering Happiness: A Path to Profits, Passion and Purpose* (New York: Business Plus, 2010).

4. *Screw Business as Usual* (New York: Portfolio, 2011) is the title of Richard Branson's latest book.

The Next Chapter

1. "Live on Purpose," *Healthways*, February 12, 2012, http://blog.healthways.com/2012/02/living-on-purpose/.

Acknowledgments

Thank you to my Digital Royalty team—each and every one of you. What a ride it's been over the past few years, and I thank you for all the lessons, successes, failures, and trust in our vision. We are more than coworkers. We're friends, family, teachers, and students to each other. Your passion for what we're doing together is unmatched and it's what fuels the future. #KeepItRoyal

A huge thank you to Chad Martin, my renegade partner in crime. I could write another book about the gratitude I have for you. Your unconditional support has been one of the greatest gifts I've been given. We will miss you, but you're always a part of the team.

Alana Golob and Jessica Smith, our group texts make my day more enjoyable. We've proven laughter can fix any situation, and I'm forever grateful for our rock-solid connection. Alana, our value exchange has always been something else. Watching your personal and professional growth over the past few years will always be one of my favorite memories from this past chapter. Jess, my fearless life managing director, I value your ability to remember my address when I do not and the millions of other things you do for the team on a daily basis with a smile on your face.

Tony Hsieh, thank you for always asking me, "Why?" Your friendship, mentorship, and now business partnership have been blessings. A wise man once told me, "If we can fix the cities, we can fix the world." Let's do this. Viva Las Vegas.

Baron Davis, your endless kindness is your greatest asset. Thank you for sharing it with me. The friendship and now partnership we have are incredibly special. We've been talking about doing something together for years! It's just a testament to our resilience and persistence. Just imagine…

Thank you, Shaquille, for all those tall lessons, including the power of remaining grounded. Our long-lasting friendship is treasured, and you'll always be The Big Social Media Center to me. I'll never forget when you called me and said in your renegade voice, "Never defend yourself. Your friends don't need it, and your enemies won't believe you anyway."

Thank you, DJ. I never imagined that a guy who goes by "The Rock" would understand me the way you do. Your motivation inspires and pushes me a little further than I think I can go every day. Clear big picture thinking, poise under duress, and knowing when not to force something out of sheer will are just a few assets you've added to my tool belt. I'm grateful.

If there were a king of renegades, it would be Dana White. I learned more from you than you'll ever know. As real as it gets. And to all the rad clients and partners I've worked with throughout the years, thank you for your willingness to experiment and take risks. Your continued fearlessness is celebrated. I'm humbled by the 1.2 million who have followed and joined this journey via Twitter over the past several years.

I'm not quite sure where I'd be without my life coach, (magic) Mary Maisy-Ireland. The personal and professional growth spurts that you've sparked were day changers and lifesavers. You should raise your rates!

My renegade book team, Kevin and Mat, must be commended for leading the path and putting up with my rookie author ways. Your talents are unparalleled. Same goes for my core team and Jossey-Bass, especially Susan Williams, my fearless editor, for believing in this small town girl from Wyoming from the beginning—and granting a few manuscript deadline extensions.

I thank the crew of supporters from my Phoenix Suns days: Steve Nash, Rick Welts, Drew Cloud, Lynn Agnello, Jeramie McPeek, John Walker, and Bill Sutton. A little healthy tension here and there is just part of the renegade culture. Thank you for the lessons and allowing me to color outside the lines without crossing them.

Elizabeth Loucheur and Heidi Burgett, thank you for traveling the world for work and exploring with me. The memories wouldn't be the same without you, and we've netted out with friendships that will last a lifetime.

Last but definitely not least, I thank my personal board of directors (you know who you are), Jaye Quadrozzi for teaching me the meaning and power of a person's intent, the three JJs, and, of course, my parents. I'm a self-proclaimed handful, and you've embraced my crazy factor. I love you.

The Author

Amy Jo Martin, a Wyoming native and Arizona State University graduate, founded Digital Royalty, a social media agency, in 2009 to help companies, celebrities, professional sports leagues, teams, and athletes build, measure, and monetize their digital universe. Digital Royalty also provides customized education programs through Digital Royalty University, which offers a variety of curricula for social media, as well as personal and business innovation. The education programs blend strategic and tactical training for corporate brands, small businesses, sports entities and leagues, individuals, celebrities, and athletes.

Martin was named one of *Forbes*'s Best-Branded Women on Twitter in 2010. She has more than 1.2 million Twitter followers (@AmyJoMartin) and travels throughout the world to speak about personal and business innovation, trends in social media, how to monetize various social platforms, how social media have redefined innovation, and how to build a personal brand by using social media.

Martin is a regular contributor to the *Harvard Business Review*, *SELF Magazine*, and *Sports Business Journal*. She and Digital Royalty have been featured in top-tier media outlets, including *Vanity Fair, TIME, Forbes*, the *New York Times, Fast Company*, ESPN SportsCenter, *USA Today*, MSNBC, and *Newsweek*.

The Digital Royalty client portfolio includes Shaquille O'Neal, DoubleTree by Hilton, FOX Sports, *SELF* magazine, Chicago White Sox, UFC, Dwayne "The Rock" Johnson, Los Angeles Kings, Cleveland Indians, New York Knicks, Tony Hsieh (CEO of Zappos.com), Discount Tire, Monte Carlo Resort and Casino, and Hard Rock Hotel and Casino.

Index

collaborative innovation using, 7;
as communication, not advertising,
opportunities, 44; democratizing
access through, 28; demonstrating
UFC brand loyalty "return" on use
of, 43–44; #GiveNASCARaChance
hashtag, 114–115; Japanese
earthquake and tsunami (2011)
news and aid through, 166–167;
Jimmy Fallon's early use of, 105; Kobe
Bryant's decision to close his account
on, 59; *New York Times* adoption of,
129; NHL Hashtag Battle on, 153–156;
Roger Goodell's sudden silence
on, 34–35; Tiger Woods's lack of
human connection on, 55; tracking
transactions on, 138; verification
system of, 128; Very Happy Person
(VHP) program use of, 161–162;
Women's World Cup Final (2011)
record-setting night for, 167–169. *See
also* Social media
Twitter Queen. *See* Martin, Amy Jo
"Twitter tutorials" requests, 1
2010 lockout situation, 34

U
UFC (Ultimate Fighting Championship)
brand: announcement on FOX
Sports partnership with, 99–102;
Boost Mobile fighters "fan phone"
approach to the, 42; Dana White's
use of social media to establish,
37–39, 43; demonstrating "return"
of Twitter use to the, 43–44; Digital
Royalty responsibilities for sharing
events of, 71; graph of conversation
spike for, 102; innovative approach
to creating the, 37; providing UFC
fighters with social media training,
39; Ultimate Fighting Championship
212 heavyweight event of, 154
UFCONFOX Sports tweet,
101–102
Ulman, Doug, 154, 162, 164
The Ultimate Fighter
(UFC programming), 37
Unmasking your motivation: barriers to,
62–63; strategies for, 63–68
US Airways, 149–152
US Airways Center, 3
U.S. senator's story, 91–93, 109

V
Value, *See* Brand value
Vanity Fair magazine, 65
Vaynerchuk, Gary, 159
VegasTechFund, 136
Veneered identities: growing public
rejection of, 93–94; of traditional
marketing, 93
Verizon Wireless, 14

DIGITAL ROYALTY

Digital Royalty was founded in 2009 by CEO Amy Jo Martin. In 2012, it partnered with two new investors, Tony Hsieh, CEO of Zappos.com, and Baron Davis, NBA All-Star and point guard for the New York Knicks.

Digital Royalty's agency division develops digital integration and social media strategies for corporate and entertainment brands, professional athletes, celebrities, sports teams, and sports leagues. It has a global reach and pioneers measurable concepts for big personalities. Digital Royalty's education division, Digital Royalty University, launched in early 2011, has become a focal point for the company.

Digital Royalty's client portfolio includes NBA legend Shaquille O'Neal, DoubleTree by Hilton, Chicago White Sox, FOX Sports, *SELF* magazine, Ultimate Fighting Championship, and Dwayne "The Rock" Johnson, among many others. The work of Digital Royalty has been featured in top-tier media outlets, including the *New York Times, USA Today, Newsweek, Fast Company, Forbes*, and *Mashable*.

To learn how Digital Royalty can help your business, sign up for the e-blast, search for job opportunities, or review case studies, visit www.DigitalRoyalty.com

Connect with Digital Royalty
Facebook: www.Facebook.com/ DigitalRoyalty
Twitter: @DigitalRoyalty (#KeepItRoyal)

DIGITAL ROYALTY UNIVERSITY

In 2011, Digital Royalty launched an education division, Digital Royalty University, which specializes in developing customized curricula in the following areas for every level and position within a company:

- Social media
- Company culture
- Business and personal innovation

The curriculum is also offered to individuals, students, and small- to medium-sized businesses online at www.TheDigitalRoyalty.com

When developing education programs for companies or individuals, Digital Royalty University works closely with each partner to establish both short-term and long-term objectives of the education program. Once those are established, university staff use an online survey to assess the skill set of each attendee undergoing training. This assessment allows Digital Royalty University to build a comprehensive curriculum to meet the needs of each student.

Digital Royalty University has a blended learning approach of in-person strategic and tactical training, as well as online sessions that include both video demonstrations and quizzes. More than one hundred modules are available, ranging from social media education to personal and professional innovation—for example:

- Social Media Overview
- The Art of Social Media Event Activation
- Emerging Platforms
- Developing a Culture Road Map
- Social Media Ad Buys
- How to Design Your Own Day
- Top iPhone Tips and Applications

Digital Royalty University training is available for corporate brands, small businesses, and individuals looking to accelerate their knowledge of social media and personal innovation. A certification program has been established to gain the Digital Royalty University stamp of approval.

Digital Royalty University has worked with a variety of brands, celebrities, sports teams, and verticals, including DoubleTree by Hilton, FOX Sports, WWE, Ultimate Fighting Championship, and *SELF* magazine, among many others.

To learn more about Digital Royalty University and how you can join the Digital Royalty University graduates, visit www.DigitalRoyalty.com

AMY JO MARTIN—SPEAKER

Amy Jo Martin has more than 1.2 million Twitter followers (@AmyJoMartin), and she travels around the world to speak on the following topics:

- Innovation and leadership
- How humanization leads to monetization
- Social media trends within the sports industry
- Social media and sponsorship

Her audiences have included Harvard Business School, Social Media Mom's Celebration at Walt Disney World, MasterCard World Headquarters, TEDx, Prudential Annual Conference, National Sports Forum, and the Design Leadership Summit in Venice, Italy, to name a few.

Amy Jo is a regular contributor to the *Harvard Business Review, SELF* magazine, and *Sports Business Journal*. She and Digital Royalty have been featured in top-tier media outlets, including *Vanity Fair, TIME, Forbes,* the *New York Times, Fast Company, ESPN SportsCenter, USA Today, MSNBC*, and *Newsweek*.

To invite Amy Jo Martin to speak at your upcoming event or organization, visit www.AmyJoMartin.com/Speaking

Connect with Amy Jo
Facebook: www.Facebook.com/AmyJoMartin
Twitter: @AmyJoMartin
Tumblr: www.RenegadesBook.com
"Renegades Write The Rules" Official Hashtag: #TeamRenegades

ROYAL BLISS

"If you fix the cities, you fix the world"

Digital Royalty recently moved its headquarters to downtown Las Vegas to be a part of the Las Vegas Downtown Revitalization Project led by Tony Hsieh, CEO of Zappos.com. Tony, who believes that if you can fix a city, you can fix the world, has privately funded $350 million to aid the revitalization. The Downtown Project is dedicated to transforming downtown Las Vegas into the largest community-focused city in the world.

Through the VegasTech fund, the funding is allocated across five areas: $100 million for real estate, $100 million for residential, $50 million for small businesses, $50 million for education, and $50 million for tech start-ups.

Typically a project of this magnitude would take more than fifteen years, but the Downtown Project is committed to completing the project in less than five years.

Digital Royalty is honored to be part of this special project and higher purpose. This is Digital Royalty's royal bliss.

For more information on the Downtown Las Vegas Project, go to www.DowntownProject.com, or follow it on Twitter: @DowntownProjLV.

Ready, Set, Pause...

We are all moving at the speed of light every day, trying to balance our professional and personal lives. Sometimes a short reset, or "pause," can make a world of difference in your health, productivity, creativity, and overall well-being. We encourage you to join in on our daily "Ready, Set, Pause" by consciously making the commitment to yourself to stop for four minutes and listen to a song, take a walk, meditate, or do whatever else allows you to emotionally and mentally reset. In reality, there are 1,440 minutes in every day, so what's four minutes? Join the conversation on Twitter by using the hashtag, #ReadySetPause, and let us know how the daily "pause" is going for you. For more information on Ready, Set, Pause, visit www.ReadySetPause.com.